Do Yourself a Favor:

Your Wife

Do Yourself a Favor:

Your Wife

By H. Page Williams

Bridge-Logos

Gainesville, Florida 32614

Bridge-Logos Publishers
Gainesville, FL 32614

Do Yourself A Favor: Love Your Wife
by H. Page Williams

Library of Congress Catalog Card Number: 73-85896
International Standard Book Number: 0-88270-204-1

Printed in the United States of America.

All Scriptures are quoted from the *King James Version* of the Bible unless otherwise identified:

TLB = *The Living Bible: Paraphrased* © 1971 by Tyndale House Publishers, Wheaton IL 60187

G1.318.FBM.m509.35230

Dedication

To my wife, Patti and our children, Perry and Plythe—
who have given me the joy of being a husband and
father—and to the glory of God.

———————■———————

Contents

Preface

A legitimate question in the minds of most men who get ready to read a book of this nature is, "What are your credentials?" My credentials come from the truth of God's Word, taught to me personally by His Spirit in fifteen years of the gospel ministry and eighteen years of glorious marriage. God has placed on my heart a message for every home, because I see so many miserable men and women who don't know how to handle their homemade problems and are searching for survival in so many false ways. Out of the spiritual discernment God has given me, I have written this book to serve as a manual for marriage.

H.P.W.

ONE

Honey, Is Anything Wrong?

The bedroom door slams, and Fred hears his wife stomping down the stairs. He is glued to the television. As he watches the Miami Dolphins huddle, he quickly opens the door, and his ears pick up the clamor of pots and pans coming from the kitchen.

They pick up a first down—but there is a flag on the play.

"Damn!" he thinks.

Fred takes a gulp of beer and grabs for a pretzel as he shouts, "Susie, go down to the kitchen and ask your mother if anything is wrong."

The Dolphins call time-out with thirty seconds left on the clock—score tied. The quarterback trots over to the sideline.

Susie drags her Miss Beasley doll down the stairs. The horn-rimmed glasses drop off of the doll's face onto the bottom step. As the kitchen door flings open, Susie says to her mother, "Daddy wants to know if anything's wrong."

"That's typical, that's just typical!" exclaims the mother, with a high pitch in her voice as she plops disgustedly down in a kitchen chair.

Susie scrambles back up the stairs, and as she drags her doll past the bedroom door, her dad cries out, "Susie? Well, what did she say?"

"She's tickled, just tickled to death," answers Susie, as she looks at the fleeting puzzled expression on her father's face before he turns back to the TV set.

"The right end catches the quarterback bomb and streaks down the sideline," yells the announcer, as the superstar stumbles over for the touchdown.

Somehow dad hears the cry of his infant son in the other room above the tumultuous noise of the television. He thinks, "Why in the devil doesn't that baby's mother do something?" And he reaches for another pretzel.

———————■———————

A friend of mine came home from his office to find his wife quietly packing her suitcases.

"Honey, is anything wrong?" he asked.

"I'm leaving you, Harry," she replied. "I've taken all I can take. I don't want to discuss it, so just leave me alone."

Harry couldn't believe what was happening. They had been married for five years and had what he thought was a wonderful marriage. His wife had seldom complained, and most of the time she was the devoted little wife he wanted her to be.

I observed another couple over a period of months, realizing that something wasn't exactly right in their relationship. For one thing, the woman kept building her husband up, saying how wonderful he was, what a good provider and father he was, and that they never had any problems. Yet at the same time, I could see signs of resentment and bitterness in the way they interacted with each other.

When a husband or wife tries to make a point that all is well and there is no problem in their household, it is a decoy. They are trying to cover up the truth which they are unwilling to face or to deal with. As it turned out, this wife fantacized a lot about another married man and was trying to cover up by making over her husband. She really loved him, but had slipped into unhealthy daydreaming without realizing it. After discussing the matter, we decided to let her husband in on it, and when she indicated to him that she had gotten caught up in an affair, he said, "Honey, is there anything wrong?"

Indeed, there was plenty wrong on his part. Actually, he was the one who let it happen. He did not feel that anyone else could possibly be interested in his wife. The implication was that no one else would have her. She craved affection and attention so desperately that when she found it in someone other than her husband, she was unable to dismiss it and didn't want to, either, because attention and affection are something every wife needs.

If a woman's God-given husband fails to provide her needs, the consequences are often critical. This particular wife was riddled with guilt feelings, hurt, bitterness, resentment, fear, anger—the whole bit—all because her husband was unwilling, or perhaps unable, to show her his love.

Maybe you are a soft-spoken guy, and never get upset, never get angry, always try to deal with family matters on a low-keyed, intellectual level. When things get out of hand and go sour on you, the self-righteous man, can always pull the family together and say, "Okay, which one of you did it?" never realizing that you are the one who did it, that it is all your fault.

For example, there's an outburst of temper. The wife takes as much as she can, and then she starts throwing things around, and they smash and break. You come up with an I'm-too-good-for-that attitude and make her feel like she's out of her mind, that she's some kind of a psycho. You never stop to think why she's doing this, why your wife is getting so upset. It may be just to get your attention. You have been utterly oblivious of her and the children—you live in your own private world. Oh, you're a good man, all right. You go to church; you don't squander the money; and don't badmouth your mother-in-law, and you stay out of trouble. But you don't do anything imaginative or exciting around the house. You seldom compliment your wife or the children or anything your family does. You don't play with the children; you don't show much tender love and affection to your wife. You go about your own carefree, clumsy, corny way, while your family simply fades off into the background.

I'm talking about reality now, and it's serious business because if you are self-righteous, you think you are so good, and yet you are not aware that your failure to become involved in your family's affairs is a serious shortcoming, a sin. You may not know what's going on in your own home and could care less. For example, the children need new shoes for school. "So what? That's the wife's problem," you think.

Your son has a dental appointment next Friday at four o'clock. "So what? The wife can take care of that; I don't need to know about it."

Your daughter has piano lessons every Tuesday afternoon after school. "I don't need to know that," you think.

Aunt Matilda is coming to visit next week, and there is a problem as to where she should sleep. "That's not my problem; that's my wife's department," you rationalize.

The dog needs his rabies shot. "So let the wife take care of the details," you say.

The neighbor's children keep coming over at odd hours and making trouble. "I'll take care of that after I've watched this football game," you reply.

The couple down the street is having loud and boisterous parties, and your wife wants to know what you are going to do about it. "You can't just go invading peoples' privacy." That's your cop-out this time. "We'll just let it go—I'm a peace-loving man."

Your wife is going to the hospital for surgery. "So why should I make arrangements for the children? Let her do it before she goes, or I'll get Mom to take care of the problem," is your answer.

The back left-hand burner on the stove isn't working properly. "Saturdays are my only days off—let the wife call someone to come fix it."

One of the children saw an insect in the bedroom and thought it looked like a termite. "I'll look later. Can't you see I'm reading the paper now?"

There's a light bulb out in the dining room. "Honey, can't you do anything around this place?"

The paperboy threw the paper on the roof three weeks ago, and it's still there. "I'll get up there next week, but I've got to see the Super Bowl today."

I asked one wife what it was that her husband was doing that caused her to want to leave him, and her reply was "Nothing." Frequently, it is what men fail to do as heads of the home that gets the family all messed up, rather than what they do.

One reason men have lost the respect of their families is that they have become spectators in the family situation. I asked one little boy what his father did, trying to learn what his occupation was, and the boy replied, "He watches."

I asked, "You mean that he is a night watchman?"

"Oh, no," the little boy exclaimed, "he just watches."

"Well, what does he watch?" I asked.

"I don't know if I can tell you everything," he continued, "but I can name a few things."

"Well, tell me," I replied.

"He watches TV; he watches Mom do the housework; he watches for the paperboy; he watches the weather; and I think he watches girls, too," he said, with an impish grin on his face. "He watches the stock market, football games, all the sports. He watches mother spank us, and he watches us do our homework. He watches us leave to go to church and PTA and shopping. He watches my brother mow the lawn, and he watches me rake. He watches my sister clean up the dirty dishes, and he watches me wash the dog. He watches Mom write letters, and he watches me play with my dog. He watches Mom pay the bills. He watches me a lot—but mainly he just watches," said the little fellow, with a note of sadness in his voice.

This dad, and thousands like him, has contracted a contagious disease I call "spectatoritis." It takes many forms.

Let me illustrate: Mr. Brown has been married for more than fifteen years. He has a responsible job, three children, a home, and a very talented wife. He gets up in the morning and begins heckling his fourteen-year-old son with something like this: "Hey, Bill, why did you leave the lawn mower outside all night? Can't you ever do anything right?"

The son replies, "You're gonna start on me again today, are you?"

"You're blankety-blank right I am. The trouble with you kids these days is that you don't ever want to do anything. I work my tail off day and night to get you all these things, and then you don't even want to help."

"The phone rang, and I forgot about the mower being outside—I'm sorry," Bill says, leaving the breakfast table with his stomach in knots.

"And don't forget," Mr. Brown shouts as Bill retreats down the hall, "I want that hair cut before this week is out!" His tightly clenched jaw reflects his inward seething. Barely begun, the day is ruined already.

This dad has the mistaken idea that earning a living is the ultimate in his responsibility around the house and that everybody else is to bow and scrape when he comes in after a long hard day. He thinks he is the only one who has any really big problems, never suspecting that each member of the family has his or her own needs and that he is supposed to help them. Instead, he always makes light of their problems and says, "I wouldn't wish my problems off on anybody," indicating that he thinks he is under the heaviest pressure of all. He never stops to think of the agony his son is going through, trying to grow up into adulthood, and desperately needing counsel and understanding and guidance rather than the rejection and criticism and tongue-lashings and grumbling that his dad dishes out so abundantly.

This Mr. Brown watches like a hawk for any additional evidence for his suspicion that everybody in his household is trying to get out of doing his job, and then he watches for every opportunity to point out the mistakes and blunders and laziness of each member of the house. On the other hand, he never watches for opportunities to be supportive and helpful when they seem down and out. He never tries to get into their world to discover their feelings, their hang-ups, their dreams, their successes, their likes and dislikes. This father could really be a blessing to his son if he would put forth the effort to find out what it feels like to be fourteen years old, what his son's particular problems are, and what he can do to help his son think them through. How did Dad handle those problems when he was that age, and what did he feel?

I pick up many clues from fathers and sons that tell me that Dad never watches for chances to talk with his son. Mr. Brown's son is naturally full of antagonisms. He is angry and resentful and rebellious, but Dad thinks it is only because the kid is lazy or no good. The boy is crying out for love from his father, but his father is so full of self-love that he has none for his son or any other member of his family, except maybe one he has picked out to show favoritism to. I see this happen so often. The father and one child have this thing going between them, and Dad says, "This is the only one of the bunch worth anything." Then he points to Bill and gripes, "He's the black sheep." Dad has given time and attention and praise to the one child who feels loved and therefore responds to love, whereas he has criticized, badgered, and run down Bill. It is no surprise that Bill is jealous, insecure, antagonistic and rebellious. All the time, Dad thinks it is the boy's fault or the wife's fault.

When the mother senses that Bill is being neglected by his father, she takes up for him, and then an unhealthy relationship is established between the mother and the son, causing him to become feminine. This makes Dad angry, and he jumps on Bill even harder, trying to make a man out of him. This makes Mom angry with Dad, and most of the time none of them knows what is going on. All they know is that it is hell around the house.

Mr. Brown could easily solve the problem by admitting that the whole difficulty is due to his self-love and his lack of love for his family. Mr. Brown is so much in love with himself that in his work, he is Mr. Bigheart—always smiling, always giving, always treating everybody with special attention. He has learned how to win friends and use people. But he is a different man when he steps into his house—everything changes. He is Mr. Grouch, Mr. Touchy, Mr. Big Mouth—all rolled into one. His attitude is, "By damn, this is my domain, and I can do as I blankety-blank please. I've had to put up with my boss, my customers, my fellow-workers, and now I want what I want when I want it, and I'm the king, so everybody better watch out. I've had to put up with all this stuff in my work, and I'm not about to put up with it in my home. I deserve some peace and quiet, and that's what I got a wife for. She's supposed to keep it quiet, have my house clean, my food prepared, my clothes washed, my house in order, my children educated, my paper ready for me, my slippers, and my pipe when I come home."

Such a husband and father doesn't know about the New Testament concept of sacrificial love, of dying to live and giving to get, of serving to be served, of losing to find. Oh, he's heard of it, because he goes to church every Sunday, but it has never registered as something a husband and father is supposed to live by. He just lets it go in one ear and out the other and gets on with the business of loving himself as always. The reality of God's Holy Word has never dawned on him to the point that he can see what a cruel and wicked person he is.

I see a lot of homes that are having problems among men who are church-going men. That problem arises out of the fact that men who go to church often become self-righteous in their attitudes. They feel like they have done their duty.

A young man attended church with the attitude, "I'll do my wife a favor by going to church with her." The church services were a little long, and they were detained in getting home for him to finish watching the last of the Golf Classic, so he became angry. The whole family became disturbed because of his self-righteous attitude.

Even if you are doing the right thing, many times it is with the wrong attitude. As a result, you are made angry, because you are kept from doing what you like—then you nullify the good you thought you had done.

Maybe you have compared yourself to Mr. Drunk or Mr. Evil or Mr. Trash or Mr. Poor or Mr. No Church. Compared to them, you are Mr. Sobriety, Mr. Good, Mr. Treasure, Mr. Rich, or Mr. Church Attender. By comparing yourself with other inferior men, you can always make your family feel guilty, and also build up your own ego at the same time. If they complain about anything you do or don't do, you can come up with, "What if your daddy was like Mr. Drunk?" "What if I was Mr. Poor, and you couldn't have all this stuff?" "What if your father didn't go to church, like Mr. No Church?" On and on *ad nauseam.*

These are but a few illustrations of marriages and homes that are sick because they're caught in the epidemic of husband-father spectatoritis. The only known cure for this cancer spreading across our country is Christ Jesus. When we men truly turn to Christ and are occupied with Him, then He will become resident boss in our hearts. Then society will return to sanity and safety and salvation, and our homes will find healing and help, and we'll have heaven and harmony and hope for this present age.

Now, if you are a normal, natural male, you have begun to protest a little at this point and think of all the idiosyncrasies you have to put up with from your wife. But we are discussing the men, and it is our desire to discover if there is anything wrong. Just think of this book as a mystery you're trying to solve: Who did it?—Who committed the crime? If you will relax, open your eyes, and hear all the evidence, I believe there will be a surprise—but happy—ending in it for you.

two

Danger Signals

There are many clues that couples give when they are having homemade troubles. When the signs of domestic discord point to rocky roads and crowded thoroughfares, we ministers know there is a collision coming. However, most men and many women are unaware of the danger signs, or they ignore them, not believing that they are on a collision course.

Here are some of the clues to watch for:

(1) When a member of the family builds the other up, but with an undercurrent of bitterness.

(2) A couple that uses a public situation to cut each other down.

(3) A husband who uses his wife as the butt of his jokes.

(4) Couples who say they have no problems and have never had a fight.

(5) A husband who calls his wife ugly names.

(6)   When the husband begins to make excuses for being away from home or simply stays away without an excuse. This is true of the wife, also, even if she is involved in worthwhile activities.

(7)   When the husband shows very little attention to his wife; when he does not show her common courtesy or tenderness.

(8)   When a husband seldom helps with any upkeep of the home.

(9)   When there is constant bickering and nagging and picking going on between a couple.

(10)   When the husband and wife both work, and he goes his way and she goes her way.

(11)   Couples that cannot discuss differences without getting into a heated argument or fight.

(12)   When the couple decides to have separate bedrooms, and when a couple has little or no physical contact.

(13)   When the in-laws are allowed to set policy or make decisions for a man and his family.

(14)   When the husband pushes off on his wife the responsibility of making the decisions or even lets her have it because she wants it.

(15)   When the children are not well-behaved and mannerly.

(16) When you feel resentment and rebellion on the part of the teenagers toward their parents.

(17) When a couple moves into a neighborhood beyond their income or seems to place more emphasis upon social acceptance and material things than upon spiritual needs of love and humility and worship.

(18) When a couple spends all their time in every activity that comes along—including church— yet never takes time to be *with* each other.

These are just some of the clues that point to areas of family life that are not being dealt with satisfactorily and therefore will eventually culminate in separation or divorce, even if it takes five to fifty years to erupt.

I sensed some of these signs in a couple some years ago and finally, one Saturday afternoon, when the wife could take it no longer, she started throwing things around the house, while the children and husband looked on in dismay, unable to believe their eyes. Here was this man's otherwise cool, calm, and collected wife, having a fit. He had to forcibly restrain her (she had finally gotten his attention) and then he said, "Honey, is anything wrong?" Of course, there were hundreds of little things that had built up over the years, and finally, she exploded. Had her husband been perceptive, he would have detected these little irritations and would have dealt with them as they came up.

"But it is humanly impossible to be able to cope with a wife, with every little detail. I work all day and can't possibly know what to do to help her or keep her from having a nervous breakdown," said the woman's husband when we discussed this in my office.

"You are absolutely right," I replied. "Of course, with only your own steam and power, you are unable to cope— but the Lord can work it in you to be spiritually sensitive to see what is wrong. Sincerity, by itself, is not enough. When we are in the dark, we need the sensitivity of God and the light of God's love to show us."

While I was taping the devotions at a television station not long ago, I was trying to present some principles in capsule form on the theme, "Men, do yourselves a favor." After each three-minute cut, the cameraman would come up to me and say, "But what about the wives? Don't they do anything wrong?" I knew that what I was saying was getting to him. He was responding in the typical male way of pointing his finger at the wife and dumping off on her the responsibility for the failure of the home to function as it should. He had a few minutes before his next job, and so while he was changing the equipment around in the studio, we discussed his question.

"Did you know that our wives are the biggest influence in our lives?" I asked. He nodded his head like he knew what I was saying and replied, "Yeah! My wife is always telling me what to do, and man, do I get tired of it!" I tried to show sympathy, but decided to stick my neck out and do a little counseling.

"Is there anything wrong in your marriage?" I asked. He answered, "Oh, no. We've been married for two years, and we get along real great. I like to have peace, so I just go along with her, so she won't keep pushing."

I sensed that he wanted to say more, but was hesitant to talk with me about it since he had already told me they got along great. So to help him out, I asked, "Does your wife work?"

"Yes, as a matter of fact, she does," he said. "She's a nurse." This gave me a big clue as to why there could be all kinds of hang-ups they would have to work through. First of all, she was better educated than he; next, she made more money than he; and thirdly, she was independent. These are matters that really need to be dealt with, especially if the man is proud—and most men are.

"What are your plans?" I asked, trying to find out if he was an ambitious young man with dreams of going places or climbing the ladder of success.

"Oh, I think I'll stay here where I am. I like this kind of work." Then I realized why his wife was pushing him. She was expecting a baby soon and would have to take a leave of absence from the hospital where she was nursing. They would have it real tight, living off the salary he was making, and she was beginning to feel the pressure, yet they weren't being able to get it out into the open. Since he was unwilling to admit that his marriage needed help, I was unable to pursue it. They will struggle with it for many years—if the marriage lasts that long—unless they're willing to admit to a problem.

This is the way many men try to handle their problems—by evading the real issues, by saying they don't have a problem, or by stubbornly refusing to open up.

There are a lot of men who will not be honest with their wives and so are passively aggressive. In other words, they get their own way—regardless of what their wives suggest or say. They tune them out and go right ahead with their own selfish desires, although they have given the impression to their wives that they have listened.

Why not just be honest with your wife and tell her you are selfish or that you don't like her suggestion, rather than giving the impression that you're being sweet by tolerating her talk?

When I say this to men, most of them say, "If I'm honest, she blows a fuse!" And I reply, "You mean you can't take the consequences of your being honest, so you take the passive way?" Most men don't realize the damage they do over the years when they treat their wives with this passively aggressive attitude. It creates a communication gap, because you have tuned your wife out so much that you don't hear what she is saying, and you don't relate. You have taken the "chicken" way, and it comes home to roost sooner or later.

This passively aggressive character, which may be you, is not performing his aggressive role in the manner God ordained, because he does not have guts enough to stand on God's Word and suffer through the stages of silence or sounds of fury. It is inevitable that your wife will become despondent and frustrated and confused. This is because you don't assume your role as the initiator and the aggressor. Your pride and your touchiness cause you to run away from your role.

A woman must have something to which to respond, because God has made her a responder. So whatever you put out, the wife responds to that. Therefore, if your wife is no good, it's because you haven't put much out for her that is good. If you have the best little wife in all the world, then you've done something right.

> *Be not deceived ... whatsoever a man soweth that shall he also reap (Galatians 6:7).*

One fellow asked me, "Why does my wife have to keep on and on and on yelling, screaming, and fussing? Why doesn't she just say it one time and let that be it?"

I replied, "Because you usually ignore her requests, you seldom listen to what she says, and so it builds up to the point where she has to explode in order to get your attention."

In the process of counseling, I have found many reasons why wives just up and leave their husbands. They take all they can take, and finally, not knowing what else to do, they decide to leave. Most men I talk with say, "If she had just told me what I was doing wrong, I would have listened."

What most of us husbands don't realize is that our wives have discussed their feelings with us dozens of times, but because we were reading the newspaper or a magazine or watching TV or were otherwise preoccupied, it did not sink in.

I was over at the Big Star grocery store, and I saw a family shopping together, and I said to myself, "Isn't that sweet—husband and wife and two children shopping together?" I thought it was so wonderful, but as I passed by the cart, which was chock-full of food, I heard the husband say, "I'll be blankety-blank if I'm gonna push this heavy cart," and he walked off. I turned around just in time to see the petite little wife struggling with the heavy basket and one of the little boys trying to help his mother.

Now that actually happened, and it displays the attitude which you may have. "It's *my* money," he probably thought, "and I worked hard to earn that money. Why should I push the buggy?" And so he left it for his wife to push.

"Honey, is anything wrong?" I heard him ask as they were leaving the store.

This is just one illustration of what men leave for their wives to push, simply because they are the victims of the villainous operation of Satan. You may chuckle if you wish, but this is one of the reasons women's backs are being broken along with their hearts, because their hero has become a heel and is little help in the home-hassle against the enemy.

Now of course, Satan is half-right. He quotes Scripture. He says, "You've worked hard. By the sweat of your brow, you worked for that money. That's the curse upon you."

And to Adam, God said: "Because you listened to your wife and ate the fruit when I told you not to, I have placed a curse upon the soil. All your life you will struggle to extract a living from it ... All your life you will sweat to master it, until your dying day" (Genesis 3:17, 19 TLB).

So Satan says. "You've got a right to take it easy. You have worked hard—by the sweat of your brow. So take it easy, and have a little fun. Do yourself a favor: buy a new car, or a new toy, or a new color television set, or a new suit. Take off and leave home. Get away from the children and the wife." That's what Satan tempts us with, and it could very well be that you are buying his line.

One of the most effective tools Satan uses is "half" truths and "sometime" truths to get a man's ego inflated so that he thinks he's bigger than he is. Thus he becomes a bully and pushes his wife and family around. If you shrug at what I am saying, then you had better be very careful that you have not been carved into crafty Satan's viewpoint.

When you bully your wife around and push her around and overpower her with cursing and anger, you are really sick. You have a sick marriage. I know a man who bullies his wife, thinking since he is the head of the home he can do as he blankety-blank pleases. He has failed to realize that his authority to be head of the home comes as a gift of God and requires his own sacrificial giving of himself to his wife and children.

Instead, he buys anything he wants for himself to play with, while very seldom encouraging his wife to get nice things. He talks ugly to her, and has made her ugly in her disposition and even in her looks. She is very insecure, afraid of growing old, and is suicidal because she is unable to cope with a husband who is blinded from seeing he is doing anything wrong. His attitude is something like this: "I've provided her with a home, a maid, children, a new automobile—everything money can buy. Now, what is wrong with that? Why is she so unhappy?" He thinks she is the luckiest gal in the world to be married to such a clever man.

He has not caught on that he himself is the cause of her unhappiness and frustrations. He doesn't realize that he bullies her and criticizes her, very seldom complimenting her or praising her, or seeing her as a person of worth in her own right, with a need for tender, loving care. He thinks a wife is a slave, and it is her duty to do this, that, and the other, without attention and praise and affection. When she does not receive from her husband what only he can give, her life becomes a disaster area, and she feels doomed, because she knows he will never change.

When you become a tyrant and put your wife down, always calling her ugly names and complaining about how she looks and what she does, and being critical of all her actions, then you are really hurting yourself, because she is a part of you, a part of your very body and being.

Man's temptation is from Satan, Satan who says, "Do it my way; use worldly means to accomplish your rule of the home."

The reason this is such a big temptation is because a woman wants to be ruled. Her great desire is to be subject to her husband, because God has ordained it to be so:

"I will greatly multiply thy sorrow and thy conception; in sorrow thou shalt bring forth children;

and thy desire shall be to thy husband, and he shall rule over thee" (Genesis 3:16).

That's the curse of a woman. And her desire to be ruled presents two basic problems. Your wife wants to be ruled and to be taken care of and protected and have someone to provide for her, so much so, that when you do not fulfill the divine order within your home, then she rebels and loses respect for you.

The other problem is that her desire to be ruled leaves her wide open to be abused by you. She welcomes authority; she wants to be ruled; and she wants to be protected by you, but you listen to Satan, and so you do some of the following things: You make demands upon your wife that she can never deliver. You overrule her on every point so that she loses her self-assurance. You make her feel like a dummy—a nobody and a nothing. You take advantage of her; you belittle her; you humiliate her in public; you aggravate her; and you badger her.

If you are a man who has succumbed to Satan's temptation, whatever goes wrong in the home, you blame your wife; it's her fault. If she doesn't respond sexually, you say she's frigid. If you are in debt, you say she spends your money. If your children are little demons, you say she's a no-good mother.

So this puts a woman in a spot, too. And what is her defense? What can she do to defend herself? I'll tell you what your wife may be doing. She may be getting sick—psychologically and physically—because it is the only way she can strike back when she is being used and abused by you, the supposedly good king. But, in reality, you are being a wicked king. Or she has to go to work to get out from under the pressure of your saying, "It's my money, my home, and you're my wife, and you've got to do this and that." Or she may take an overdose of pills to attempt suicide, because she has lost all respect for you and for herself. Or she may have an affair with a man or several men. (If you blame her for this, you're out of line.) Or she may become a bitch and crabby, or she may try to run away or she may sue for divorce. All of these are ways your wife uses as a means of defense.

This is why it is so easy for Satan to break up your home—because you are not assuming your God-given right to be a good king. These are the temptations Satan puts in you, and you must recognize the source of your trouble and use the weapons God has given you to deal with the conflict. These weapons are listed in Ephesians 6.

> *I use God's mighty weapons, not those made by men, to knock down the devil's strongholds. These weapons can break down every proud argument against God and every wall that can be built to keep men from finding him. With these weapons I can capture rebels and bring them back to God, and change them into men whose hearts' desire is obedience to Christ (II Corinthians 10:4-5 TLB).*

So you seldom get around to realizing that God has delegated to you the authority to be the head of the home. And the way the home goes is the way you make it go or the way you let it go. If your home is fouled up, it's your fault, man. Put the blame where the blame belongs.

I know what some of you men are thinking. You're saying. "But you just don't know my wife!" "But you just don't know my situation!" The question is, Who are you going to believe? The Word of God and what He says? Or are you going to believe what society says? The Word of God says.

> *That is how husbands should treat their wives, loving them as parts of themselves. For since a man and his wife are now one, a man is really doing himself a favor and loving himself when he loves his wife (Ephesians 5:28 TLB).*

Jesus Christ is the example of the way a family should be together or relate to each other. In Ephesians 5:2 it says:

> *And walk in love, as Christ also hath loved us, and hath given himself for us an offering and a sacrifice to God for a sweetsmelling savour.*

Christ's love was sacrificial, and it went up to God as a sweet-smelling savor. Most of your kind of love in the home is such that it comes out stinking—just the opposite of what it should, because you are selfish. But what God says is, "If a man loves his wife, he really loves himself."

Now the world says, "Men, do yourselves a favor, and take what's coming to you. Take your wife and use her. Take another man's wife and use her. Take your friends and use them. Take your job and use it." The world says, "You only have one chance at life, so grab it, take a good hold of it with gusto. If you see that something is fun, then do it. If everything else and everyone else is doing it, then do it. If you must lie, then lie. If you must cheat, then cheat. If you have to work, then work." A man with the above attitude actually is working hard in a frantic search for happiness. His whole life is oriented around the question, "Is it making me happy?" But that is fleeting happiness that never leads to permanent happiness.

Ephesians gives us an example of the kind of people that we have in our homes today. Ephesians 4:19 begins with a relative pronoun, who. And that pronoun, who, refers to a man whose "mind has been blinded" and "whose heart has been hardened," because he has been listening to Satan. These are men "who being past feeling, have given themselves over unto lasciviousness, to work all uncleanness with greediness." Such men are actually employed in a frantic search for happiness that always slips through their fingers.

There are a lot of men who will work ten times as hard trying to do something wrong or get out of a problem in their job or a problem because they are involved with other women, than they will in trying to save their own marriages. And that's real confusion, when a man labors so hard at trying to evade taking care of his home responsibility.

To one man who had a problem in his home, I said, "Here is a good book for you to take home and read." The book was *The Christian Family* by Larry Christenson. He took the book reluctantly, because it was about an inch thick. His eyes almost bugged out at the size of it. He was used to reading the comic books, maybe the newspaper or a western or a magazine—nothing very serious.

However, he did take the book. The next day or so I was talking with him and his wife, and I asked if he had opened the book. His wife answered for him. "No," she said. "He went home and watched the Atlanta Falcons for three hours and said that he didn't have time to read the book." Now this says to me that he was slow in the mental department. Here is a man whose home is in jeopardy. He is liable for his home. He is having problems with his wife and with his children. And yet he doesn't have time to read or study to learn how to cope with them because of other things, which he allows to crowd out his family and separate him from them. He was unwilling to take the time—it wasn't that he didn't have it. Recreation was more important to him than his responsibility. If that man really wanted to do something about his problem, he could solve it very quickly by simply changing his attitude.

I often talk with men who say, "When my wife changes her attitude, then I'll change mine." But from God's point of view, men are to initiate love, and the male leader is to initiate the reconciliation. It is not a matter of giving in; it is a matter of being honest and assuming the lead in your God-given responsibility. Your home may be in terrific danger right now because you are not taking the initiative to bridge the gap, to heal the wounds, to make amends. God the Father took the initiative in reconciling us to Him, because He loved us so much. That is the way love is—it is aggressive; it is spontaneous; it takes the initiative, neither asking What if? nor demanding its own way.

> *Love ... is not irritable or touchy. It does not hold grudges and will hardly even notice when others do it wrong (I Corinthians 13:5 TLB).*

If you have a problem at home, don't run from it or evade the issue, encourage discussion. In the process of encouraging discussion in the home, be willing to listen to what your wife or children have to say. Accept the consequences of your mistakes. Be willing to get outside help if necessary.

All a man needs to do to have a great deal more happiness and bliss is to love his own wife.

In this chapter it has been my intention to stimulate your spiritual being into activity, to cause you to ask, is there anything wrong in my marriage? To help you not take for granted the family situation as you have been viewing it, but to view it from another perspective—to see it as God sees it. Hopefully, you have felt some activity of the Holy Spirit of God working in you as you have been reading these pages. I'm asking you now to be willing to listen some more to the still small voice of God as you continue into this next chapter where we seek to learn just what is wrong with what we men have been doing. Ask God the Holy Spirit to open your eyes to see who you are. An essence of tragedy is to have lived, and yet never to have known who you were. Your identity is based upon your relationships. When your life is lived "in self," you are a nobody, but "in Christ," you are a somebody. When you lean upon the Holy Spirit, He becomes your invisible means of support. If this experience with the Lord does not happen in you, it cannot happen through you.

The home is to be the church in miniature, and someone has said that the mission of the church is hatching, matching, and dispatching. There is the hatching of children from the husband and wife relationship, then comes the matching of their children with Christ and a life mate. This relationship is dispatched into the relationships of this world with others to share, to give and receive. This is God's divine program, and when we come under the leadership of His Spirit, then we become instruments of love and peace and joy.

What I am asking you at this point is not that you see completely what's wrong in your marriage, but that you should *want* to see what's wrong under the love and light of the Holy Spirit.

THREE

Honey, What's Wrong?

I agreed to talk with a man one weekend, and I could tell when he picked me up that he was quite nervous and hesitant to discuss whatever it was that was on his mind. Finally, after holding it in as long as he could, he blurted out, "My wife got angry with me last night, and she took the children this morning and went to her mother's. What I want to know is why. What's wrong with me?"

He honestly wanted help, and what a joy it is to have a man truly seeking for guidance in his marriage—a very bitter pill for most of us fellows to take. How humiliating it is for a man to have to ask for help. But a very large percentage of men have never been taught a single thing about the divine order in the home and how they are to be the spiritual leaders—the prophet, the priest, and the king.

Oh, we get plenty of slick magazine advice on how to be the kind of men who conquer their women and how to influence our wives and use them. And we even get the idea from other men that their marriage is going great 'cause they have just told their wives how it is, and if they don't like it, they can lump it. But that is misinformation, and it has caused irreparable damage in thousands of homes.

Let us go back now to the young man's question, "What's wrong?" He was willing to come with his wife for several counseling sessions to work through what it was that was wrong. During the first session the wife said, "I don't believe you love me."

"Yes, I do, honey. Why do you think that I'm here?"

"I don't know, but if this is the way you show love, then I'm sorry, but I can't take it," she stated angrily.

"What in the devil do you mean by that?" he asked.

"When you come home, you go straight for the booze and don't even ask how things have gone with us," she declared.

"We've been having trouble in the business, and I need something to relax my nerves," he said.

"But does it take two or three doubles?" she snapped.

"It does when you're screeching and yelling at me, damn it. I just can't take your nagging and bellyaching everytime I come home."

"Well, if you wouldn't drink so much, I wouldn't get so upset," she vowed.

I could detect the anger and fear of the wife as she talked, and I saw that Mr. Jones was full of self-pity and looking for a liquor crutch to run from the real problem.

"Why do you indulge so heavily in alcohol?" I asked. "Are you hooked?"

"Oh, no," he quickly replied with an obvious degree of uneasiness. This was my first clue to Mr. Jones' weakness and the strong possibility that he just buried his head in the bottle. Of course, after he had gotten enough false courage from the liquor, then he would try to deal with his home problems—but by this time, the wife was furious and ready to explode. So instead of talking through and listening to each other, they fought.

While they fought, the children were huddled in the corner developing all kinds of complexes and anxieties. If Mr. Jones had been man enough to answer honestly my question about his drinking problem with a response like, "You're right—I am beginning to get hooked on that stuff, because I don't know how to handle this tiger of a wife of mine—" If he had just admitted that he did drink too much, then we would have been well on the way to making a correction in his marriage, but instead he did what most weak men do; he denied it.

He was not a parent, but a parrot, echoing the bitterness and anger of his wife.

"I don't drink too much, Preacher. I just use the stuff to calm my nerves and help me relax every evening. Is there anything wrong with that?"

"Do you feel you need that to keep you calm?" I asked.

"Oh, no!" he denied. "I just drink because I enjoy it, and nobody is going to tell me when I can drink and how much. So tell her to get off my back."

This was his way of saying, "Change the subject," and it was easy to see his self-pity and rebellion and stubbornness. I thought, "Boy, this guy is going to be a tough case to crack. Lord, help me here. What do You want me to do?"

It popped in my mind to change the subject and ask Mrs. Jones a question.

"What do you feel love is, Della? I mean, how do you interpret your husband's love to you?"

"I'm not sure I know what you're asking," she replied, "but I feel if my husband loves me, he will show an interest in me and take time to learn what I like. And he will compliment me when I wear something that makes me look especially nice. Is that what you mean?"

"Exactly," I said. "How do you feel your love is expressed to your wife, Mr. Jones?" I asked. He thought for a moment, like it was a real tough question, and then finally mumbled, "I work and make a damn good salary, and I buy her everything a woman could want—she is always wanting something—and so I think I show her love by letting her have what she wants."

I could see a big gap in what Mrs. Jones said and what Mr. Jones said. They were miles apart in their interpretation of the way love is expressed.

I turned to Mr. Jones and asked, "Do you feel there is a possibility that you could change your attitude about how to express your love to Mrs. Jones and begin giving her time, attention, affection, and praise?"

"No way," he blurted out.

"Hallelujah!" I shouted. "You've finally told the truth."

"Preacher, you're getting me confused. I thought you wanted me to say I'd change my attitude," he confessed.

"I do want you to change your attitude, but I also want you to stop appeasing and start saying what you really feel. You see, marriage is based on truth and purity and fidelity, and if you can't be honest with your wife or yourself or anyone else, then you are really in trouble."

"You don't understand, Preacher," he said. "If I told my wife the truth, she'd be throwing fits every five minutes—so I just keep my mouth shut."

"That's the trouble with us men, Mr. Jones. We're too yellow to go through a crisis or battle of the wits, because we know we are wrong and are too stubborn to admit it, so we just give in and make our wives look like dirt.

"By being honest, Mr. Jones, I mean I want you to tell the truth about yourself—your feelings, your attitudes, your pride, your self-pity, your fears, your hang-ups—and then watch your marriage begin to heal. Why? Because your wife will respect your honesty much quicker than your rationalizations and excuses and sublimations."

Mr. Jones still looked dazed and puzzled. He had always thought it was sissy to admit that you had a problem. "Let me give you two an assignment," I said.

"You mean I've got to wash the dishes every night or make up the beds?" he asked, viewing me suspiciously.

"Oh, no, Mr. Jones, nothing that easy. I'm not asking you to do KP. I'm asking you to start being honest with yourself and your wife."

"Give me an example," he said.

"Okay, here's what I want you to do. Instead of running for the bottle for support when you come home at night, run to your wife. Tell your wife—the girl God gave you for a helper. Share with her your anxieties at the office. Tell her how uncertain you were when you hired or fired that person on the job. Share with her your feelings of loneliness when it looks like everybody is plotting to push you out of your position. Tell her you can't handle it, and you need a word of wisdom from someone you know cares for you and loves you and isn't trying to do you in."

"Preacher, if I did that, she'd laugh me out of the house. I told her a problem I had one time down at the office and in two minutes she had the whole thing solved. Now, you know it's not that easy."

"No, sir, I don't know. In fact, I suggest to you, Mr. Jones, that your wife's answer was right and that she solved it so easily that you were embarrassed and unwilling to admit it and say 'Thank you, honey, for your brilliant mind.'"

Mr. Jones was all shook up because he had never heard of this kind of counseling, and furthermore, he had always thought that wives were dumb animals to be used as domesticated servants—never someone to confess to or admit your faults to. He was always suspicious of his wife, thinking that she, too, was out to cut him down. What he had never gotten through his thick skull was that his wife was his greatest asset and that she truly was the answer to his problem. All this time, he had seen her as the problem, and now he was beginning to get a faint glimmer that maybe he was the problem.

"Will you do this assignment for me, Mr. Jones, and then let me know how things work out at our appointment next week?" I asked.

"I'm going to be honest with you, Mr. Williams," he responded. "This is all so damn new to me, I don't think I'm going to like it."

"That's great," I said, grinning from ear to ear. "You're beginning to catch on. Believe me, I know you are not going to enjoy it at first. But if you do it, I can guarantee that before too long you and your wife will be experiencing a much greater depth of love and happiness."

There were so many hang-ups in this one little family that it took many months to even get around to some of them, but after about a year, I was talking with Mr. Jones, and he said, "Preacher, I really did think you were out of your mind when you wanted me to admit that I was wrong and to let my wife in on my inner feelings about myself and my work. But I can't believe what a change has come over my wife since I've been sharing all my intimate thoughts and fears with her. She is so sweet and thoughtful—and very seldom nags or gripes anymore. Since I have seen myself as head of my home by giving and not getting, I have found more joy in living, and I can't wait to get home to be with my family. Before, as you pointed out, I was using the alcohol as a crutch, and it wasn't holding me or my family up. In fact, it built me up to let me down. Since I've been taking the initiative in saying, 'I goofed,' I've found my wife and children being more relaxed and ready to admit their faults and mistakes without me having to point them out. I'll confess this though, Mr. Williams, I still get angry when my wife tells me what I should do or shouldn't do."

He grinned when I replied, "Thank you for being honest!"

———————————■———————————

Our wives exercise an influence over us for good and for bad. We must learn to discern the different ways our wives influence us. God holds us accountable for our decisions and for the way our homes go.

The Adam and Eve story should have taught us something about marriage. Satan knew just how to get to Adam, and he really "ribbed" him and robbed him by going through his wife, Eve. She was the one the serpent used. Knowing her nature to be curious, cunning, crafty, coy, and cute, he used her influence to convince Adam to lose his soul by listening to his wife instead of the Lord.

Now hold on to your hats, men. Don't jump to conclusions and say, "I knew all along it was my wife's fault that I'm in all this trouble!" We can't get out of it that easily. God made you to be the decision-maker, and He made you to be obedient to Him, and to glorify Him, and enjoy Him. And He gave you your wife to give you some spice. God used a woman named Mary, the espoused of Joseph, to begin a new generation. Joseph would have been off-base had he not listened to that sweet innocent young girl when she said, "Honest, I haven't been fooling around." And he would have been in trouble had he not listened to the voice of the angel who said, "That which is conceived in her is of the Holy Ghost ... and thou shalt call his name Jesus." A man must realize that God often uses his wife to communicate to him, and because Satan uses her as a tool also, it is a man's responsibility to figure out when it is God and when it is Satan. You and I can't put the blame on Jane any longer; that is why man must be up on the Word and not down on the wife.

There is one truth I am beginning to discover, and hopefully, your eyes will be opened to it also. Although marriages are made in heaven, it was God's plan for them to be lived out here on earth. For that reason, the moment the marriage vow is sealed, we begin a period of adjustment that lasts as long as we live in these "earth suits" of ours. The Word says, *For the unbelieving husband is sanctified by the wife (I Corinthians 7:14)*. Our wives are sent by God to make believers out of us.

I have a sneaking suspicion that you guys are like I am—if you will admit it—I don't like to be corrected by my wife! Doesn't it rankle every time your wife gives you a suggestion or tries to correct you or shows you where you have made a mistake? Isn't that one of the reasons why you clam up when you come home from a hectic day on the job? Because, instead of sympathizing with you, she shows you where you have goofed, or she gives you a solution to the problem that is so simple and you can't stand being shown how dumb you are. And don't cop out with that, "Well, she didn't do it sweetly," attitude. Where we men miss the point, however, is not a question of who is right or wrong—it is a question of our ego. We are so afraid of getting our ego stepped on that we go into our "silent routine" until the storm has blown over. Naturally, this saves our face and makes the wife look like a fool. But those who are wife-wise understand that this is God's way of getting to us. It is best to let your wife do her thing—to serve as a mirror to help you see yourself—to help you mature. That's the way God operates.

I get bombarded by human and satanic viewpoints so heavily that I am often insensitive to the gentleness of the Spirit of God to the point of being "dead" in conscience and unconscious of the "real me." But God uses the lips of my wife, whom He has given special influence, to speak to me, to awaken me, to mature me. My big thing is to rebel. My rationalization department quickly registers a negative response to any correction which my wife offers.

For example, my wife received a revelation from God to begin talking directly to those toward whom she has ill-feelings—to tell them what is bugging her—to get it off her chest and then give them the freedom to handle it in any way their maturity or lack of maturity allows them to. This has two beautiful effects: 1) it keeps her from having to tell everybody else her feelings; and 2) it relieves her from the burden of carrying it around in her heart. When she told me

I should do it, I thought that it was an excellent revelation, but since God hadn't given it to me and since she had failed to use her own revelation on occasions, I rebelled against it until I could get further confirmation directly from the Lord. I was pulling the old male ego trick—insisting that if God had anything to say, He would tell me first and then I could pass it on to the other members of the family.

On more than one occasion—more like hundreds of occasions—I have had to be taught very elementary truths from my own children. For example, I spent one whole Saturday putting down some new tifton sod in our little fenced-in back yard where we were keeping our puppy poodle so he would not run away.

The next morning, Sunday, I put the puppy outside and crawled back in bed to get a couple more winks before getting ready for Sunday school. When I got dressed in my Sunday apparel, I opened the back door and saw our poodle, all covered with mud. He had been having himself a ball, pulling up half of the sod that it had taken me one whole day to put down. I got red in the face and started yelling and fussing and grumbling at the "dirty" dog. My fourteen-year-old son poked his head out the back door and very quietly said, "Dad, are you praising the Lord?"

During breakfast, I was still grumbling, and Patti, my wife asked, "Sweetheart, are you praising the Lord?" I angrily replied, "Give me two more minutes." Our family was trying to learn this principle of God's Word so beautifully presented by Merlin Carothers in his books, *Prison to Praise, Power in Praise,* and *Answers to Praise,* but as you can see, it takes the whole family working together to help each other mature in love and faith and truth.

That same day, my wife had baked a cake to take to the church's annual picnic and had left it on the dining-room table while we had gone visiting. When we arrived back home to gather up our goodies for the picnic, my wife saw her beautiful devil's food cake half gone. It didn't take but a second for her to know who to blame—the poodle had struck again. She started fussing and scolding, and we all chimed in, "Mother, are you praising the Lord?" Her reply was, "Give me two more minutes!"

There are a lot of men—you may be one of them—who are unbelievers whose wives are being used by God to correct them and help them in their growth or in their salvation. I had one unbelieving husband tell me, "My wife tears into me like a tiger, and I ain't about to listen to her on any subject unless it can be delivered in love."

Some men are truly cruel to their wives, and then when the wife can take no more and does fly off the handle, we come up with this self-righteous cop out. You say, "Well, what about how cruel my wife is to me?"

"Whatever you see in your wife that you dislike or are repelled by is there because you have not taken time to deal with it. You blame her instead of yourself," I told one man who was complaining about his wife. If I came to you face to face and told you boldly what you were doing wrong, you would blow-up, just as this man did. But if you ask God to reveal it—He will show you. I'm not saying it will be easy. But the real men of our society are those who have guts enough to let the light of God's righteousness shine in their hearts and come under God's authority and submit to His leadership—then and only then will men become the men God intended them to be.

God has revealed to me that one reason that we are having so much difficulty in life today and so many, many problems from so many areas of life is because the home is not what God intended it to be. And since you are the head of your home and divinely ordained to take that responsibility, I'm laying it on you. You can shrink from it if you want to, or you can say anything you would like by way of rationalization, but you are going to have to understand and respond to God's plan for your life as the head of the home unless you want to be miserable.

FOUR

Who's At Fault?

G od is divine, and man is human, and Abraham was no exception. In fact, Abraham, the father of our faith, can show us a few tricks in how to be a heel.

God told Abraham to leave his own country and his own people and go to the land to which He would guide him. This he did in fine fashion and noble faith—what a hero! However, *There was at that time a terrible famine in the land: and so Abraham went on down to Egypt to live (Genesis 12:10 TLB)*. This is very subtle, but if you look closely, you will find that Abraham took it upon himself to leave the place where God put him. Why? Because there was a famine—a big problem. The minute things got tough, he decided to move on to greener pastures, carting his whole family with him. Sounds so modem, so human, so much like us.

Meanwhile, we notice that Abraham had failed to think through his decision to move down to Egypt and had failed to discuss all the possibilities with Sarah, so he missed out on the counsel his wife could have given him—had he asked. Again, mirrored in this ancient story of a hero, we see ourselves. Like Abraham, we get a bright idea, and figuring that our wives will find a few flaws in our thinking, we just up and do it, putting our whole family in misery.

Caravaning down to Egypt, Abraham got to looking over the delicate lines of his elegant wife as she swayed rhythmically with the motions of the camel below her, the sunset beyond her, the smile upon her face, the long flowing hair behind her, and the thought came to him that she was lovely to look at. So, as they were approaching the Egyptian border, he asked Sarah, his wife, to tell everyone that she was his sister. He tried to cover up his big mistake with a half-truth. (She was his half-sister, but she was foremost his wife.) His tricky thinking sounds so mod.

> *"You are very beautiful," he told her, "and when the Egyptians see you they will say, 'This is his wife. Let's kill him and then we can have her!' But if you say you are my sister, then the Egyptians will treat me well because of you, and spare my life!" (Genesis 12:11-13 TLB).*

Why? Why was Abraham so willing not to protect his wife? Because it is human nature. As they were moving along the trail, Abraham casually said, "Honey, let's play a little game!" "Oh, I like games," she might have replied. "Good," said Abraham. "Now here's the way it goes. You tell everybody that you're my sister, and don't tell them that you're my wife, and see if they can guess."

This was Abe's game to save his own skin. But see how cruel he was to Sarah? While Abraham was getting all the promotions, his poor little wife was getting inducted into the harem of King Pharaoh. Now, if there is one thing that a woman does not like, it is to be used. She wants to be loved and respected as a person and not just a body. She believes her body is for her husband alone, and this wife-swapping is out of her league.

Now, your question at this point might be something like this: "Well, if she is so smart, why doesn't she tell Pharaoh the game is over and walk out? After all, she doesn't *have* to play if she doesn't want to."

But this is where our male minds get a little twisted. It is just one more method of putting the blame on Jane instead of admitting that it was our idea in the first place. Think of the humiliation and exposure Abraham put his wife through, simply because of his pride and ego and self-preservation. Now you say, "Boy, that was a dirty deal for him to pull, but I don't do that." But I say we do it quite often and don't even realize it. Begin today to notice how many times you blame your wife for things that you get yourself into.

One young man was telling me about how poor his wife was with the management of the home. He said, "We are in debt up to our ears, and I kept asking her if there was anything wrong."

"Do you let your wife handle the money in your home?" I asked.

"Oh, yes," he said. "But that is going to change. She got us into this mess and it will take me five years to get us out. She can cook and clean and work and take care of the children—but boy, is she lousy in the management of money!"

If you are reading this and don't see anything wrong with that line of thinking, then chances are, you are doing the same thing. You see, in the first place, the fellow should never have passed the buck to his wife. If a man is going to need financial consultation, let him go to a banker and not push it off on his sweet little wife. In the second place, he is being unfaithful to his wife by not believing that God will provide and that God has a divine order for the home, and he is out of order. "Whatsoever a man soweth, that shall he also reap" (Gal. 6:7). So, if a man sows disorder, he will reap disorder sooner or later. If the man continues to grumble and think, "What a bum deal I got. Just think of all the girls I could have married," he has truly missed the grace of God.

This little episode in the life of one man's family—Abraham's—was used not to dishonor or discredit him in any way, but simply to show how cruel even the best of us can be. If we ever put on our halos, thinking how lucky our wives are to have such great guys, then we are in the midst of making them miserable. Pray that God will open our eyes to see just what kind of creatures we really are.

I am not suggesting that our wives are all that innocent and always sweet little angels. They can be contentious, like Abraham's wife, Sarah, but that still does not excuse us from our responsibility as the spiritual and sacrificial heads of our wives. Remember, it was this beauty queen of Abraham's who said,

> *Since the Lord has given me no children … you may sleep with my servant girl, and her children shall be mine (Genesis 16:2 TLB).*

Now, no man in his right mind is going to believe his wife is sincere when she says a thing like that, but Abraham wanted to appease her and have a little fun on the side, so he accepted her noble sacrifice.

That, however, was his big mistake, for here again one of God's servants bit the dust by "hearkening unto the voice of Sarah," and not unto the voice of God, Now, hundreds and hundreds of years later, the descendants of Abraham's sons, Israel and Ishmael, are still fighting, and will be till Christ returns.

Although God forgave Abraham for this mistake, and blessed him by making him the father of many nations, Abraham still had to reap what he sowed—a principle we fellows have difficulty comprehending.

I am saying many things here, but we are following the line of thought that our wives are a tremendous influence for good or bad and that we—the men, the head of our wives—must discern, in the spirit, which influence we are going to hearken unto. This, I must repeat, can only come about by our agreeing with God that we are sinners, that we cannot handle this tall order of God's in our own power, and therefore we die out to self-will and call on the Holy Spirit of God to give us direction and guidance.

What I am asking of you men and of myself is that we put a stop to blaming our wives for our mistakes and that we see that God has given our wives to us for our help.

But remember that in God's plan men and women need each other (I Corinthians 11:11 TLB).

A wife is responsible to her husband, her husband is responsible to Christ, and Christ is responsible to God (I Corinthians 11:3 TLB).

And the Lord God said, "It isn't good for man to be alone; I will make a companion for him, a helper suited to his needs" (Genesis 2:18 TLB).

I was talking with a man the other day, and asked him, "Is there anything wrong?" He said, "My wife is a nag, a hag, and a bag—all rolled into one."

"Boy, oh boy, you have really fouled up, haven't you?" I said.

His eyes got big and he asked, "What do you mean?"

I asked, "Do you know why your wife is a nag?"

He said, "Is it 'cause she doesn't like the way I do things?"

I said, "You're right! You have made a nag out of your lovely wife because you haven't done what you should have done when you should have done it. If you would take care of your business as head of the home, then she wouldn't have to be a nag."

"Do you know why she's a hag?" I asked.

He said, no, real innocent-like.

I said, "It's because when she does get dolled up and has her hair done, you don't even notice it. You don't pay her any compliments. You're not aware of it, so she says, 'What the heck!' She gives up, and doesn't try anymore. That's the reason why she's a hag."

He said, "Well, why in the world is she a bag?"

And I said, "Because she is frustrated with you as the head of the home. She doesn't know anything else to do but to eat her way out of the problem, and that's the reason that she's fat. You've made her that way. She's overweight because you haven't given to her what she needs as a woman. If you don't make her feel like she's beautiful, the most beautiful thing in the world, she gets frustrated and uses eating as an alternative—and it's all your fault."

The cruelty of a man toward his wife comes in a variety of ways. I am thinking of a family whose husband is in the medical profession. He provides all the financial needs of his wife and children, but denies them the greatest need of all—his time. This man did not set out to hurt his wife, nor to willfully neglect his role as father to the children. He simply found himself caught up in the pressures of the medical profession, and instead of opening his eyes to the first responsibility of his role as husband and father, he cast himself into the role of the "needed physician" who makes others well. This demand of his profession upon his time could easily be controlled, but his ego drive has blinded him from seeing the cruelty of not becoming involved with the wife of his youth.

You were united to your wife by the Lord. In God's wise plan, when you married, the two of you became one person in his sight. And what does he want? Godly children from your union. Therefore guard your passions! Keep faith with the wife of your youth. For the Lord, the God of Israel, says he hates divorce and cruel men. Therefore control your passions—let there be no divorcing of your wives (Malachi 2:15-16 TLB).

This man and many like him have divorced (separated) themselves mentally and physically from their families because of their passion for praise in their profession and their drive for fame and fortune. Their cruelty comes by their saying, "But I can give them everything money can buy, and they lack for nothing." What is needed is what money can't buy—a father's time and attention and appreciation and understanding. This husband, overly involved in his profession, might also rationalize, "But see what a great contribution to the health and welfare of mankind I am making."

Live happily with the woman you love through the fleeting days of life, for the wife God gives you is your best reward down here for all your earthly toil (Ecclesiastes 9:9 TLB).

If we men would work as hard at our marriage as we do at trying to impress the socially elite or our fellowmen, we would all have spiritual and lively homes. No matter how successful a man may be in his profession or business, if he fails in his home-business, he has truly missed his whole point for existing, namely to glorify God.

God's glory is man made in his image, and man's glory is the woman (I Corinthians 11:7 TLB).

The teaching of this Scripture is quite deep—but in a very simple way we could say that when a man obeys God, trusts God, loves God, and serves God, then he is the glory of God. This holds true of the wife. When she obeys, trusts, loves, and serves her husband, then she is his glory. But there is one catch, which most men have difficulty seeing. Unless we become the king, the prophet, the priest, the aggressor, and the initiator in marriage, then the wife has nothing to which to respond. She can only glorify her husband to the degree that he glorifies the Lord God. This is why so many women these days are not feeling fulfilled and are on the woman's lib kick. We men could set our wives free if we could glorify God in the way we were designed in His Grace and Plan. Those of us who ignore this principle and are unbelievers and unfaithful and living in our ivory towers of pride and prejudice are, necessarily, cruel husbands.

In the process of dealing with family problems, I have found that men are very touchy. We have to be unbelievably delicate so that we don't hurt their tender feelings. They are so easily disturbed that instead of dealing directly with the problem, we have to evade it; we have to go around it; we have to use all kinds of subterfuge in order to make a point.

Why are you touchy? Because of your pride. You don't want to admit that you have a problem, and you are unwilling to deal with it.

The question I have is this: Is there anything more important than saving and salvaging your marriage? You say, "Yes, everything is more important," when you evade the issue.

Your ego says, "I'd rather lose my marriage than change. I'd rather lose my marriage than repent. I'd rather lose my marriage than be found out. I'd rather lose my marriage than admit that I have failed or admit how slow I am."

Watch ye, stand fast in faith, quit you like men, be strong (I Corinthians 16:13).

If your marriage is in trouble, you can always rationalize and blame someone or something else. Let me give you a few examples of what you may be doing to rationalize. You say, "The reason I can't get along with my wife is because of my job. I have to spend so much time at my job, and she just doesn't understand. So it is my job that causes us to have problems." Or you may say, "My problem is that my wife is a grouch." Or you'll use your health. "I'm a sick man." Or you'll talk about your in-laws, or you'll blame the children or the neighbors or society or you'll say, "It's the war—I had to be away from home a year." Or you'll blame the church. "She is always wanting me to go to church." Or you'll blame the Lord. "God let me down." Sometimes the minister gets the blame for marriages failing, either because he didn't care enough or he was too nosy.

You can always blame anything and everybody, never opening your eyes to see that it is your own pride, your own selfishness, your stubbornness, your own rebellion, or lust, or indifference.

Let me tell you now what it is in men that causes so much difficulty in the home. It is pride. Pride keeps you, in the first place, from admitting that you have a problem. With the people that I talk to, it is usually the man who is oblivious to the fact that there is any trouble at all in his home life.

There is a couple that my wife and I have known over the years. This family is in serious trouble simply because the husband will not open his eyes to see and admit that there are some things he needs to change in his attitude and ways. He has failed to assume responsibility in making decisions, thinking he was being the good guy by letting his wife do it. He has lacked feelings for his wife's needs as a person and has caused her to become distorted in her thinking. He is such a proud man, he will not admit that there is anything seriously wrong with his marriage. The attitude he displays is, "Even if there was something wrong, it could not possibly have anything to do with me."

Pride also keeps us from admitting that we can't handle the problem even if we admit that we have one.

In the third place, pride keeps us from dealing with the problems, simply because we don't want to make it any better. We may be "one up" on our wife, or we're fooling around and we don't want to do anything about getting it straightened out. So, it is pride then that keeps us from admitting our weaknesses, and it pains us to read about it even in a book like this, because we cannot accept the truth.

I have received some comments and some feedback from people in regard to this book, which I feel I was inspired by God to write. I was quite nervous about this book, because of the seriousness of what needs to be said, and the reluctance on the part of men to hear the message.

My wife received a phone call the morning after I preached about some of the thoughts contained in this book. The call came from one of our members who had listened to our services on the radio. She said, "I'm going to sue your husband for plagiarism for that sermon he preached last Sunday." My wife, of course, was quite shocked, and her immediate reaction was, "Oh, no. Here we go," because the lady was so serious as she spoke. The lady said, "Yeah, I've been preaching that sermon for thirty years, and he stole it from me."

I had a feeling that a lot of the wives were not understanding the principles I had been presenting because I heard a lot of comments from the women like, "We're gonna get it next." They were getting a little uneasy about my spending this much time on the men, so they assumed that they would get a double portion. But that wasn't true. In fact, the truth of the matter is, that if men did their part as head of the home, there would be little need for me to say anything to the women. So I will not, and I am going to assume that you men will take a cue from that and will follow through with these principles.

However, there is a portion of Scripture that says, "Wives be in subjection to your husbands." I have taught that, and it is a truth, and believe me, there is a need for wives to be in subjection to their own husbands. But men, I have to tell you another truth; a woman cannot be in subjection to a jellyfish, to a man who has no backbone, to a man who simply appeases, to a man who evades the issue, to a man who postpones decisions, to a man who is passive in every phase of his life. Wives cannot be in subjection to "nothing." So I think when you assume the initiative, and take your role seriously and begin living as you should, then your wife will have something to which to respond and will be happily in subjection to you as unto the Lord.

I heard another comment from a man who had been exposed to these principles, but he had divorced his wife some years before, and he said, "It's not always the man's fault. Men often do everything they can to maintain their home and keep it going." I say if this does happen to you, and you are divorced, do not try to rationalize it or blame anyone or any circumstance. This is not the way to handle it.

Yes, it is true that according to God's order there is no place for divorce, but neither is there a place for hate, bitterness, rebellion, murder, lying, etc. But human beings come short of the glory of God by sinning, by doing these things. Divorce is on the same level. It is not the unpardonable sin. God forgives divorce on the same basis as He forgives any other sin that you commit. If you repent and confess, then God forgives and cleanses us from all unrighteousness. Accept it, and then forget those things which are behind, and press on.

If you have become the victim of a broken home through the powers of Satan, trust that God has forgiven you and then accept the divine truth of what we are trying to teach. It is the man's responsibility to be the head of his home, and if it disintegrates, it is because he is not functioning properly as the head of the home. He is not being the prophet, the priest, and the king as God divinely ordained him to be. Just accept that as a truth and then follow through with it, because there are a lot of holes in your argument saying, "I did everything that I could possibly do to save that marriage." I could show very easily that you are not the spiritual leader of your home in the way God intended you to be. If there is one area in which we fall down the most, it is in this area. We let our wives take the initiative in the training and discipline and teaching of the children, and as a result, the home is in difficulty and may be near being dissolved. This is not because the wife is incapable of doing the job, it is because we men have copped out on our responsibilities, and dropped out of our role as student and teacher.

FIVE

How to Get Right

When I went over to St. Francis Hospital to visit the sick, there was a sign out front. They were remodeling the hospital, and the sign read "Danger, Hard-Hat Area." And I kept seeing that and it kept making an impact in my mind that there was a message there somewhere, and then when I began to think about us and our responsibility in the home, it came to me that this was a danger area because it's a "hard-head area." You and I are stubborn and unwilling to change, and so it becomes a danger area whenever we do not respond to teaching of God's Word in regard to our being the priest of our home. When you catch yourself praying, "Lord, change my husband," you know there is something wrong somewhere. Who really needs to change? You, the husband, are the one who is stubborn and doesn't want to change. When you fond out that it is your responsibility to be the priest through giving of yourself, here is what happens: You get cold feet, cold chills, and a cold heart. You rebel against it, because it involves more than you are prepared to give, namely, your ego.

Your pride or your egocentricity has to be dissolved, and so you fight with all your might to hold on to your ego, and you keep looking for other ways to find peace and prosperity and glory for your home. But there is no permanent glory and peach and prosperity for your home apart from your being the divinely ordained priest fulfilling the sacred office that God has given you.

If you are not careful, you will find yourself rebelling against your wife. If she asks you if you have paid certain bills, you explode angrily, "That's my problem. I'll take care of it." If She reminds you to come straight home from work, you stop by the corner bar. If she asks you to listen to Johnny's problem, you become angry and say, "You have more time than I do. Why don't you do it?"

If she asks you do decide what you are going to do for Christmas or Thanksgiving, you rebel. If she asks you to listen for the baby while she does something, you get angry—especially if you are watching a football game on TV.

If she asks you to help with some of the chores around the house, like emptying the garbage, or fixing a leaky faucet, or trimming the hedge, or painting the bathroom, or washing the car, or mowing the lawn or whatever—you rebel. A wife can give you a lot of things to revolt against. Why do you rebel? You are stubborn. It's your pride and selfishness. You don't want to be henpecked. You lack an understanding of your role, and so you become vindictive.

If your wife could talk to you, she would say, "Honey, what's wrong is that you are childish in your behavior. You are so afraid of being henpecked, and that isn't even my intention. Actually, I want you to make the decisions to pay the bills, to discipline the children, to take the initiative in our spiritual life. You don't do what I want you to do and even try to hurt me to pay me back."

If you would listen to your wife, she would continue, "Honey, what's wrong is that you don't help around the house with all the things that need to be done. You leave everything for me to do while you go off wherever men go to get out of their responsibilities. Sometimes you even stay home, but just say, 'I'm too tired, and I have a right to be lazy if I want to!'

"Honey, what's wrong is that I'm losing my respect for you because you don't discipline the children. You always say, 'I don't know how,' or 'I don't want to,' or 'That's not my job.' But, darling, it is your role as the father to teach and train our children in God's Word. Why do you push it off on me? It tears me up to see you so unconcerned with the care of the children, because before we were married, that's all you could talk about. 'I'm gonna have a house full of kids,' you would say.

"Did you marry be just to produce your children and train your children and care for your children while you go your own selfish way? Sure, you take Johnny to Little League, bit I get the feeling it's more to show off your offspring than it is to be with him and teach him something. I'm afraid what he is learning is how ugly is dad can be when the team loses or things don't go his way. You show your son off, but don't show him attention at home, helping him with his homework or school problems or the problems of growing up. You don't seem to take an interest in showing him how to do things. Sure, you tell him what he out to be doing, but very seldom do you get involved in his world. Yes, you try disciplining our teenage daughter by telling her, 'Betty, remember now, you be a good girl and protect your family name. Don't let anyone see you doing anything wrong—you know the way people talk.'"

We man are guilty of not knowing how to discipline our children, something that every father should study and learn how to do. We cop-out on that by saying, "Every book I read is different, and nobody knows the right way, so I'll just do it my way and let it go." This is the typical male approach to these things, and it's what's wrong with our marriages. We take the easy way, using the assumption that it really doesn't matter what we do, so we don't do anything. But it is our responsibility as head of our home to train and discipline our children so that they can be free—this is the right motive for discipline. Children who are disciplined by their fathers are healthy and whole of mind and body and spirit.

I talk with men all the time who bad-mouth the way youth are today, but they conveniently forget what sorry fathers they have been. They sat something like, "The trouble with this world today is that these young kids don't know how to work. They rebel and go around the country—cutting down their country and letting their hair grow. They ought to be cutting their hair and letting the country grow." Fathers who talk like that wouldn't begin to see that it is all their own fault. Fathers have taught this to their children and don't even know it. They thought all they have to do is tell a child something and he'll do it. Children learn more by feelings an d attitudes and examples than by telling. The Bible says,

"Train up a child in the way he should go." There's a whole lot more to training than simply telling.

I have talked with a lot of teenagers and young adults, and they say over and over, "If Dad and Mom just would be *fond* of each other, what a difference it would make!" When Dad does not show love to his wife and does not exercise any self-discipline, then there is little likelihood that his children will be strong, healthy, and wholesome when they grow up.

Heartache after heartache is experienced in this country every day because dads are so slow, so stubborn, so rebellious. Father after father whose family is in trouble says, "I thought I was doing right. I was sincere in what I was doing, but what can I do now? It's too late." I'll show you in another chapter that it is not too late and that there is a solution and a way out of our dilemma. But right now I would like to point out a few more things that are wrong.

When a man does not show love to his wife—when he rebels against her and his role as the head of the home—when he gets his own selfish way, but gives the impression to those watching that he is listening—his whole family is fouled up. The trouble shows up in the teen years and early adult life of his children.

One young man in his early twenties was about to lose his marriage, and as we talked, I discovered that he actually hated his father because his dad was this kind of character who is passively aggressive. He gave the impression that he was listening, but then did as he well pleased. He appeased his wife and was a mealy-mouthed man, never taking any active part in the home life. The son reacted to this attitude of his father and over-reacted to the point of becoming a tyrant. Instead of keeping his mouth mealy as his father did, he talked crudely and became a bully. His father made no decisions—so he made all the decisions without consultation or consideration of his wife. His father seldom had any sexual relationship with his mother—so this son treated his wife as a sex object, completely domineering her. The son was quite confused, for he thought if what he was doing didn't work and what his father did was wrong, then where was the answer?

The point I am trying to make here is that each generation falters, because we fathers do just like Dad or just the opposite. Thus it goes, back and forth, generation after generation. If we as fathers knew the impressions we were making on our children and could see what the results were going to be, we would put much more time and effort into learning *how* to be the kind of father and husband God wants us to be.

You may be a husband or father who tries to discipline his family by withholding love, but you cannot afford to do that as a policy of getting tough, because it leads to very serious situations. Discipline involves much more than a spanking every now and then or a talking to or a withholding of something. Discipline is a process of teaching principles of life by example in the way you handle your day-to-day problems and how you face life in general.

Most men feel very uncomfortable in the role of spiritual leader and have been hiding behind the skirts of their wives.

We have to come on out into the open, accept our responsibilities, and do what God intended us to do.

I was in a home some years ago and the wife was complaining about having to pick up after the mess the children made when they had a snack or took a bath or played a game or whatever.

I said, "What does your husband do?"

" Oh, he does the same thing," she replied. "He fusses at the children for what they do, but he's the worst one."

I said, "If Mr. Day would teach the children to respect their mother by showing respect for her himself and consideration by picking up his things, then you would not have that problem."

One father complained, "I'd talk with my children more, but they're never here. They are always gone or doing something."

I said, "You can change that very easily!"

"How is that?" he asked.

"All you have to do is play with them, help them with their homework, wash the evening dishes with your teenage daughter, get your son to wash the car *with* you, things like that."

"Oh," he exclaimed, "after I've worked all day, I just feel like reading the paper or watching TV. I don't think I could do that."

You see, as long as we men do what we feel like, not taking the extra effort and energy to be with our children, then we will continue to have these deep-seated problems and chaos in our homes. Not only do we men do what we feel like, we don't even have a good attitude about the good things we do, resenting every minute we are not watching that ballgame or are not in the woods hunting or not in our workshop puttering around.

A couple came to my office in one of the churches I have served, burdened down with anxieties and angers and animosities. They poured out their story of their teenage child rebelling—taking drugs, stealing, wild parties, lustful pleasures in sexual activity—the whole bit. They wanted to know what they could do. I turned to the husband and asked, "How much do you love your wife?" He looked surprised and a bit annoyed since he had come to talk about the kid. He felt uneasy talking about himself.

"I love her—I provide plenty of money, and I work my tail off for this whole blankety-blank family. You know what I mean, I give them everything money can buy. Now, you answer me—how can a kid go out and do something like that to his dad, after all I've done for him?"

I tried to get him back onto the subject, and so I asked, "Mr. B., how do you and your wife get along?" He still was quite upset, and I could tell he was beginning to get touchy.

"Well, I'm going to be honest with you, Pastor. We get along fine as long as my wife doesn't bug me. But boy, when se starts pushing me, I get up-tight and go get a few 'belts.' I know that's wrong, but I can't take that eternal nagging."

I could see his wife beginning to boil and her face getting red, and she was biting her tongue. "Every time I'm late for something, she starts in on this, 'You-never-have-time-for-me-and-the-kids,' business. Doesn't a men have any time he can have for himself, too? I work long, hard hours, and I don't need to be punching any clock. So what if I'm a few minutes late for some idiotic thing she wants to do?"

By that time Mrs. B. was about to explode, and I was beginning to get a pretty good picture of Mr. B's attitude, so I said, "In other words, you and your wife don't always get along too well?"

"That's right, Preacher," he retorted. "But like I said, if she would stop hounding me and jumping on me and nagging at me, then we'd have a little peace and quiet around the house. But what's this got to do with our boy, Pete? Man, we're in trouble, and we need some help."

"Do you have other children?" I asked.

"Yeah," he grunted. "Tell him, Sarah. I always forget those things."

I could feel Sarah was bleeding inside, but she managed to compose herself long enough to tell me the ages and names of their other three children, all younger than Pete, the one in trouble.

"The point I want to make, Mr. B.," I continued, "is that the best thing you can do for your son Pete and all the other children you have brought into the beautiful world is for you and your wife to get along."

I could see Mrs. B. was beginning to relax a bit as she saw me getting into the real problem. Mr. B. hadn't quite caught the drift of the conversation nor the connection between his attitude toward his role as husband and father and that of his son's rebellion. "May I ask you a few more questions, Mr. B.?" I inquired.

"What I want to know," he quipped, "is it gonna get me out of this mess that dumb kid of hers has got me into? Man, I've got a good name in this town, and I go to First Church every time I don't have something else to keep me from it, and I'm a member of the Rotary Club, and I coach one of the Little League teams. By the way, we ain't lost a darn game yet. I work hell out of those little rascals. That should help you out some, huh, Preacher?" I grinned, although my stomach was about to turn.

"By the way, Preacher," he went on, "what were those questions you were gonna ask?"

"Well, Mr. B., you've already answered most of them," I commented. Then I looked him straight in the eye and asked, "Do you know the Lord Jesus Christ?" He had a very puzzled look on his face and said, "I already told you I go to church every time I can work it in. Hey, you ain't gonna start on that religious stuff now, are you? Man, I don't need no preaching today. All I need is for you to tell me what I can do to talk some sense into that crazy kid of Sarah's."

He looked at me and grinned again and said, "by the way, Preacher, I know you like football, and I managed to get my hands on some extra tickets to the Florida-Georgia football game. I'm gonna give them to you for helping me out, and I might even come to your church sometime. Now, come on, you gotta help me do something about this problem."

Inwardly, I was praising the Lord for this cruel and vulgar man who was so full of pride that he was nauseating and because he had fouled up his home and his own life. I was thinking, "Thank You, Lord, for this man, and thank You for loving him through me—because You know I can't love him. Thank You for showing me now how to help this man come to a saving knowledge of Your grace and to trust in You as his Lord."

While I was praying that prayer of praise, I saw Mr. B. put his head in his hands, and after what seemed like minutes, I heard him begin to weep. Mrs. B. looked up with an expression of hope and moved her chair closer to him and placed her hand on his shoulder. I felt a tenderness of love, and then he looked up with tears streaming down his face, and he sobbed, "Preacher, I guess I've made a fool of myself, haven't I? Talking like I been talking, trying to cover up what I know must be sin in my heart. I don't know what's come over me, Preacher, 'cause I ain't never cried before, except the time my dad died and left me all alone when I was thirteen, and then I cried out under the trees where nobody could see me."

"Mr. B., do you realize that you are a sinner?" I asked.

"Well, I thought I was a pretty good guy when I came in here, but all of a sudden, I'm beginning to see that my heart's as black as the shoes I got on. Yes, I know I'm a sinner."

"Did you know that the Lord God has done something just for you that will make that old black heart of yours just as white as snow?" I continued. He thought for a moment and then commented, "When I went to church last Easter, I remember the preacher there saying something like we needed to praise God for raising Jesus from the black tomb of death where He was because He had died for my sins. But to tell you the truth, I didn't understand it then. What does all that mean?"

"Here," I said, as God revealed a Scripture to me, "let me read from what God has said."

> But God showed his great love for us by sending Christ to die for us while we were still sinners. And since by his blood he did all this for us as sinners, how much more will he do for us now that he has declared us not guilty? Now he will save us from all of God's wrath to come (Romans. 5:8-9 TLB).

"You mean as bad as I've been to my family, and as selfish as I've been living, He's going to let me go free?" he asked enthusiastically.

"He will on one condition," I answered.

"Well, if it means giving up my booze, I don't think I can do that," he replied.

"No, that's not it," I said.

"I'm gonna level with you, Preacher. I like going to church once in a while, but if I've got to go every Sunday, then forget it," he blurted.

"No, that's not it either," I said. I saw him perk up a bit, and I understood those were a couple of hang-ups that he knew he couldn't just decide to stop and start, and I appreciated his honesty.

"If that's not it, then what is the condition for me to get this sin out of my heart?" he asked. I had turned to Romans 10:9-10 in the Living Bible, and began to read:

> *For if you tell others with your own mouth that Jesus Christ is your Lord, and believe in your own heart that God has raised him form the dead, you will be saved For it is by believing in his heart that a man becomes right with God; and with his mouth he tells others of his faith, confirming his salvation.*

When I stopped reading and looked up, his face was aglow, and I knew he had begun to catch the drift of the grace of God for his very own life, and he said, "You mean that God's not asking me to change, but that He loves me just as I am and that all I've got to do to be let off the hook is believe that God raised Jesus from the dead?"

"That's right," I said. "Would you like to accept Him right now as Lord of your life?"

I looked at his wife, and she was so excited, she looked like a referee who had just signaled a touchdown. My heart was pounding, because I knew that if he humbled himself to trust Christ alone for his eternal salvation, then he could also trust Him to take care of each of his daily problems, no matter how had they seemed, even this one with his son Pete.

"I've decided, Preacher. Yep, I've decided," he exclaimed. I didn't have to ask what his decision was because there was a sweet smell of victory in that little office, and I know the Holy Spirit had scored, even with this very proud man. "I'm gonna do it, I'm gonna let Jesus come into my heart, and I'm gonna let Him be the King," was his triumphant cry. I was thinking "Hallelujah!"

Save us, O Lord our God, and gather us from among the heathen, to give thanks unto the holy name, and to triumph in thy praise (Psalms 106:47).

We knelt together, he and his wife hand in hand, and I asked him to pray this prayer and to believe:

Lord, I confess that I am a sinner. Thank You for dying for me, and thank You for forgiving me my sins. Come now, Lord Jesus, into my heart. Thank You for coming to live in my heart, and thank You for giving me Your Holy Spirit, and thank You for giving me everlasting life. In Jesus' name, I pray— Amen.

SIX

Under New Management

A man was having difficulties with his two teenage boys. One of the boys got in trouble with the law, so while I was down at the courthouse trying to give them some moral support and trying to minister to their needs, Mr. Smith asked, "Page, why is Mike giving me so much trouble?" I knew this was going to be an opportunity to witness to the authority of Christ, and so I thought, "Lord, I don't know what to say here, so I'm depending on You to give me the words to say."

"Mr. Smith, may I ask you a few questions about your relationship with Mike?" I asked.

"Sure," he replied, but I could tell he wasn't too comfortable with the thought of my prying into his private affairs.

"Does Mike seem to disrespect you on occasion?" I queried.

"Not *seems* to," Mr. Smith countered, "and not just *on occasion*. He *never* shows respect. I just don't know what

I'm going to do with that boy. He doesn't come in on time, he's letting his hair grow and won't get it cut, he's laying out of school and will probably fail—Man, I'm just fed up with his smart ways. I think I'd be glad to see him in jail just to get him out of my hair."

By this time, I was picking up some feelings of animosity from the father, and I knew that there was definitely a backlog of friction and anger stored up between the two.

"What is your relationship to the Lord?" I asked. I could see his face change from the previous angry red to a shock white. He kept shifting positions, and when he recovered from the shock (most men don't expect or like that kind of question), he blurted out, "Well, Preacher, I don't see what that's got to do with Mike and his being down here in court."

He was telling me to back off in as polite a way as he knew how, but I like to get right to the problem, so I answered, "Mr. Smith, it makes all the difference in the world. Would you say that you and the Lord are on good terms with each other?"

He exploded with curse words. "I'm in no mood to talk religion now. You sure got a lot of nerve. What are you trying to prove?"

Realizing that I had hit a sour and sore spot, I thought, "Lord, I've got an angry man on my hands, so I thank You for touching this man and using me to speak to him, but please don't let him hit me." I saw Mr. Smith with his fist clenched and I looked him straight in the eye and said, "I'm not trying to prove anything, Sam. I just wondered if you had talked with the Lord about yourself and your problem with your son. Do you know why you are so up-tight?"

What Mr. Smith did not know was that I had talked with his son on several occasions and he had told me about how his dad had threatened him and beat him, how his dad had been fooling around with another married woman, how his dad treated his mother with disrespect and disgust, how his dad would get drunk and stay gone for the weekend and how the family dreaded his coming home because he was so mean and cruel, how he felt rejected and unloved, and how he felt that his dad almost resented having him around.

"Yeah, I know why I'm up-tight," he grumbled. "It's because I've got a dumb kid in court today while I should be out working, and he's costing me money and time. After all I've tried to do for that boy! And on top of that, you ask me if I've talked with the Lord. What can the Lord do about this? What this smart kid needs is to stay in jail a few months. Then I bet he'll straighten up. But if he comes home, I'll kick the tar out of him."

"That doesn't seem to do any good, does it?" I asked. "Haven't you already tried that?"

"You trying to tell me, Page, that prayer will do more than a kick in the rear?" he asked with a puzzled look.

I realized that he was being sarcastic and yet there was an outside chance that he might really want to know, so I took him seriously and answered, "I'll tell you what I do believe. If you admit to your son that this thing is too big for you, and that you have not been right with the Lord or with your son, and that you want to get on your knees with Mike and ask God Almighty to help you all work this out—then within a few weeks you guys would have this problem whipped."

He still had a puzzled and startled look on his face, as if a door might have opened to a whole new world—one that he had never believed existed and one that he did not want to explore because he knew he would have to change.

"I'll be _____! You *are* crazy. You mean you want me to admit that some of this stinking mess is my fault?" he asked.

"No," I replied, "I want you to admit that it is *all* your fault, and in fact, it *is* you—*you* are the problem."

"You know _____ well I'm not about to buy that garbage," he retorted. "This kid has a mind of his own, and he has always given me trouble."

"How did you handle him as a two- and three-year-old child?" I asked.

"Preacher, you ask the most stupid questions," he shouted. "Hell, I can't remember that far back. Besides, I wasn't home much—you know I have to make a living. I can't do like you. You're home all the time, aren't you?"

"Thanks, Lord, I needed that," I thought to myself. Mr. Smith is like a lot of us fathers. When we shrug the role of authority in child care, for whatever reason, then this God-given quality becomes distorted, and it obscures the divine order for our freedom and fairness.

God has established order for this freedom and fairness in the prohibitions of the ten commandments, but it is the positive fifth conimandment that is the cornerstone of human freedom. "Honor thy father and thy mother." This means to give respect to the role of authority found in the parental office. Since we are children of God, then we as His childrern are to honor His Authority, whether it is doled out to us like we want it or not. God is always fair and completely just, so when a man is "controlled" by the Holy Spirit, he is able to respect the authority of God, thus enabling him and qualifying him to exercise authority himself. This principle of authority is given by God in his sovereign providential care for the protection and freedom of individuals, homes, and nations. Therefore, if we fathers fail to teach this concept to our children either by precept or example, then surely disintegration, disorder, and destruction will be inevitable in this government of home and country. Mr. Smith was a good example of a father who was beginning to reap disorder and disobedience because of what he sowed while his children were youngsters.

"I am not going to stand here and let you tell me that this whole blankety-blank mess is all my fault. Don't you preachers have anything better to do than stick your nose in other people's business?" Mr. Smith complained.

Since I had asked God for protection from a punch in the nose and since I had gotten into the subject this far, I felt led to proceed with caution. "Sam, if I watched you plant watermelon seeds and then imitated you, what do you think would be the results?"

Without any hesitation, Mr. Smith answered, "You would have watermelons come up just like mine."

Then I asked, "If you are disrespectful and disobedient to your Heavenly Father and your son imitates you, what do you think will be the results?" He looked a little white around the mouth and then replied, "I don't like what you're pointing out to me, Preacher, but I think I'm beginning to see what you're getting at. You mean if I don't recognize the authority of God over my life, then my sons won't recognize my authority over them?"

"You said yourself, Sam," I reminded him, "that Mike never shows you respect and has been unruly all his life. That's because you didn't take time as a father to teach him to respect the role of authority while he was a youngster."

"Well, I'll be damned!" he responded. "That's what I thought I was doing when I beat hell out of him and took him to Little League and forced him to do what I said."

"Do you ever bad-mouth the government?" I asked.

"You know I do. I'm in business for myself, and every time I turn around, it's more taxes and more papers to fill out. And besides, while I'm working my rear end off, the government is handing out my tax money to these lazy bums on welfare."

"Well, what about your taxes that go to pay for law enforcement officers, and this court your boy is in now, and the jail he'll be put in?" I asked.

"That's another thing," he said. "If those cops would just do their job and stop chasing me around every time I run a red light or speed or park overtime, I wouldn't mind."

"What do you think about the Armed Services?" I asked.

"I think that's a gyp," he said in a huffy tone. "Me getting my _____ shot up so these kids can run around my town stealing my equipment just so they can get another 'trip.' Man, I don't know what this country's coming to."

I answered, "It's not what this country is coming to, Mr. Smith; it's what's coming to this country."

"Whadya mean by that?" he asked.

"I mean that the Lord is coming to this country, and when He comes into your heart and my heart and we surrender to His authority, then this country will be in order and in peace and in justice," I replied.

"I'll be damned if you're not beginning to make sense, Preacher," he admitted, "but I'm gonna be honest with ya. I ain't gonna surrender to no Lord now. I'm a young man, and I got too many blankety-blank things I enjoy doing."

"There's a lot I could say about that, Sam," I commented, "but let me ask you one question. If you don't come under the authority of the Lord and surrender to His will, how do you plan to get your boy out of this trouble he's in? And what about your other children?"

As I talked with Mr. Smith, I had a strong feeling that he had not been taught this concept of authority as a child, because I could see that he was miserable and mangled in his motives and morals.

"That's what you preachers are for, isn't it?" he said. "Aren't you guys supposed to play with the kids and teach them this stuff?"

I felt this was a good time to inject a little deeper idea into the conversation, and so I replied, "The respect for authority has to be learned early in life, and this is the responsibility of a father. As your child grows into maturity, he will know how to respect the role of authority in his scoutmaster, or his schoolteacher, or his football coach, or his law officer, or his drill instructor, or his pastor, or his president. This is a home job, and since you are ordained of God to be the head of the home, it falls on your shoulders." I opened my New Testament and read from Ephesians while he sat quietly and listened.

Children, obey your parents; this is the right thing to do because God has placed them in authority ...

And now a word to you parents. Don't keep on scolding and nagging your children, making them angry and resentful. Rather, bring them up with the loving discipline the Lord himself approves, with suggestions and godly advice (Ephesians 6:1,4 TLB).

"I thought you preachers spent all your time at church. But here you are, preaching a sermon down here at the courthouse," he responded with a smile on his face.

I breathed a sigh of relief and said under my breath, "Thank You, Lord."

"I'll tell you what," Sam said as his lawyer turned the corner with Mike by his side. "Me and the boy will come to see you tomorrow, and we'll see if we can't start getting me straightened out."

He did come by the next day, and we began a series of counseling sessions that proved to be a very fruitful experience for that family. Mr. Smith came to know the Lord on a personal basis, and as a result, his wife and his children eventually saw his change from rebelling against God and his family to accepting the divine authority and order for him as a husband and father.

Mike was a bit skeptical at first, as was his mother, when Mr. Smith told them he was trusting Jesus and looking to Him from now on. But Mr. Smith took the Word of God to heart and listened to Hebrews 12:2:

> *Keep your eyes on Jesus, our leader and instructor.*
> *He was willing to die a shameful death on the cross*
> *because of the joy he knew would be his afterwards;*
> *and now he sits in the place of honor by the throne of*
> *God (TLB).*

As Sam began to imitate Christ's example, being willing to die out to self-love and willing to become totally involved in his family life, then he, too, began to reap the joys of a place of honor in the eyes of his wife and children. As Mr. Smith became more and more involved in the life of his family and the larger family of God, he learned that there was a constant battle going on between God's kingdom of righteousness and Satan's kingdom of evil and destruction. He learned that this conflict was being fought inside him in his soul and that he needed constantly to be on the alert, to watch out, to take inventory, to make use of the cross principle of dying out to self.

> *Watch out that no bitterness takes root among you, for as it springs up it causes deep trouble, hurting many in their spiritual lives (Hebrews 12:15 TLB).*

He learned that the more he learned, the more fierce were the temptations and attacks of the enemy, and that the enemy used very subtle tactics to hinder his witness as a spiritual leader in his home.

I saw Sam one day after a Bible class and he said, "Page, I know what I am now!"

"What is that?" I asked.

"I'm one of those die-hard batteries!" he exclaimed. "My old nature to rebel and resent my wife and children keeps coming back, Page," he said. "The old self keeps coming back alive."

"I know what you mean," I commented, remembering that even after years of Bible doctrine and theology, I was myself resisting the work of the cross in my outer man. This outer man is my natural nature to be self-sustaining, self-motivating, self-sufficient, self-loving, self-righteous. In other words, I (ego) like being "individualistic," and it is very, very difficult letting go of the comfortable position of ruler of my own life and destiny. I know this to be true in my own experience, so I know it was certainly true in the life of Sam, who had so far to go in learning the ways of God.

The ways of God are always hard to learn, even for those Bible heroes that we amateurs have made more heroic than the Bible itself. I'm thinking now of the character of Jacob who required a lifetime of being "stricken" by God to finally wise up to the way God operates in this world of His. It is inspiring to me to read about the ancients who, so like myself, learned through their follies and circumstances of life that the providence of God alchemized them into "saints" and fathers of our faith. It was by their faith that they pleased God.

> *And these men of faith, though they trusted God and won his approval, none of them received all that God had promised them (Hebrews 11:39 TLB).*

We dads become the heroes of our children, but unless they see us struggling with the authority of God rather than shrugging the authority of God, then we will have falsified their faith in us and we will have become a "deceiver" like our father the devil.

> *Our earthly fathers trained us for a few brief years, doing the best for us that they knew how, but God's correction is always right and for our best good, that we may share his holiness. Being punished isn't enjoyable while it is happening—it hurts! But afterwards we can see the results, a quiet growth in grace and character (Ephesians 12:10-11 TLB).*

When we begin being trained by God, it is so easy to slip back into our old shell where it is comfortable. The outer man is the vessel for the Holy Spirit in the inner man. But when we imitate Satan, then we trap the Holy Spirit within and we depend upon our own cleverness and quickness and intellect and eloquence and emotions, thus choosing to disobey the authority of God. On one occasion, Jesus said to the Jewish leaders who wanted to argue the point,

> *Why can't you understand what I am saying? It is because you are prevented from doing so! For you are the children of your father the devil and you love to do the evil things he does. He was a murderer from the beginning and a hater of truth—there is not one iota of truth in him. When he lies, it is perfectly normal; for he is the father of liars. And so when I tell you the truth, you just naturally don't believe it! (John 8:4345 TLB).*

So I knew what Sam meant when he said he was a diehard. Mr. Sam Smith is not by himself in this—I know another man who was rebelling against the authority of God and therefore found himself up to his neck in homemade problems. As a substitute for the pleasure and joy he should have gotten within his household, he frantically sought for pleasure in various extramarital sex experiences. Whenever men do that, they always come up with a poor substitute and end up with misery compounded. It was so in this man's case, for he lost his job, his family, and his friends. That was a very high price to pay for a few fleeting moments of pleasure.

> *Watch out that no one becomes ... careless about God as Esau did: he traded his rights as the oldest son for a single meal. And afterwards, when he wanted those rights back again, it was too late, even though*

he wept bitter tears of repentance. So remember, and
be careful (Hebrews 12:16-17 TLB).

God has given you a right woman to fulfill all your needs, but if you walk out on her and God, then you lose your right to your inheritance and to be her authority. If you have traded your birthright of authority for just a passing moment of pleasure to satisfy a biological or emotional urge, then you have truly betrayed your wife and your children and even yourself.

When a man is overtaken in any fault, there is a way out of the situation. Many miss it because it is so simple a solution. Understand that God loves you just as you are, and that Christ has paid for your sin. The work of Christ on the cross has provided a right standing with you and God—but you have to recognize it and believe it and respond to it.

If we confess [admit] our sins to him [God], he
can be depended on to forgive us and to cleanse us
from every wrong. [And it is perfectly proper for God
to do this for us because Christ died to wash away
our sins] (I John 1:9 TLB).

First of all, we must be obedient to what God says we should do. Most men I have had to deal with on this subject feel the way to handle their problem is to give a substantial amount of money to the church, but that isn't it. Instead, admit to God that you are out of line. It's as simple as that. There is no need to bargain with God, no need to beg God, no need to pay God off with some flurry of religious activity. Just say, "Okay, Lord, I did it, and I'm in the wrong." You don't even have to come up with bitter tears. In fact, you

85

might even feel good about having been unfaithful, but God wants to hear you admit that it is wrong, that you have sinned, that you are a manufacturer of sin. In the second place, you must realize that God is not going to give you some nasty job to do to make up for your carelessness and sinfulness. There is no need for that, since all the wrath of God has been dealt with "in Christ" when He bore all our sin on that cross at Calvary.

If you are a man who has severed his relationship from the family of God, who has betrayed himself and is in the pigpen imbedded and embittered in the slave market of sin— a spiritual imbecile—then imbibe the Word of God and be not drunk with wine, wherein is disorientation, but instead be filled with the Holy Spirit. When you confess, God cleanses with the blood of Christ, and that pigpen soul becomes a holy temple for Christ's Spirit to take up residence in and to rule your mind, your emotions, your will, and overrule your old nature to lust and egomania.

Why not take a moment right now to get this problem settled and solved—this problem you have gotten yourself into? Maybe you've been unfaithful to your right woman; maybe you've denied your role of authority in your home; maybe you've become overinvolved in business or caught up in a vicious circle of undercover work—trying to cover your bets with stolen money from illegal and illegitimate deals. Maybe you're committing the terrible sins of worry and fear and hate and vindictiveness and self-pity and jealousy and on and on. You can commit one more sin right now and that is rebellion and stubbornness, but if you do, then you will remain in your misery until you decide to confess it. This is the biggest complaint I hear from wives—they say we men are too stubborn to admit our faults and too rebellious to listen when we know they are right. You could begin right now doing yourself the biggest favor of your life by opening up to the Word of God and giving yourself as an instrument of God. Repeat this prayer in faith:

Lord, I confess that I am a sinner. I invite You now to fill me with Your Holy Spirit. Hallelujah! Thank You. In Jesus name, Amen.

I overheard a couple of men talking in the hall of the church one Sunday and this is what I heard:

"You know I haven't always been a church attender. Ever since my wife and I were married ten years ago she has been nagging me to go with her and the children to church and to talk with a minister. I thought ministers were creeps, but finally I got fed up with the wife nagging and decided to see what was so important that a minister had to say to me. I went to his office a lost man and came out saved. Do you know it's the first time in my whole life that I've been at peace? I mean really at peace with God and my family and even myself. That is one time I'm glad I listened to my wife." As they walked down the hall, I heard him ask, "Has your wife ever tried to get you to talk with a minister?"

Wives are placed in a very awkward position in that they are to come under the authority of their husbands. Their spiritual lives and protection from the satanic forces are dependent upon their husbands, so when we fail to offer the proper authority and spiritual direction, then they must suffer the consequences. It is therefore no wonder that wives are anxious for us to see the light and to see the cruelty of our neglecting the role of spiritual authority. We men leave our wives two alternatives—they either have to suffer quietly the wicked abuse of a husband too selfish for words, or they have to nag and rebel and fight for their rights.

If you are angry at your wife for wanting you to take the spiritual authority of your home, then you are a wicked and miserable excuse for a man.

> *You husbands must be careful of your wives, being thoughtful of their needs and honoring them as the weaker sex (I Peter 3:7 TLB).*

It is not your wife that you are fighting against when you try to deny her the spiritual protection of a godly man; it is God Himself. For God has ordered the man to be responsible for the wife and responsible to Christ. Therefore, I can tell you unequivocally—you are the loser if you rebel against the law of God. And I can tell you just as certainly that if you come under the authority of Christ and take up your responsibilities as spiritual head of your wife, then you will be the winner.

Jesus said, "I come not to be served, but to serve." It was when Jesus "knew that the Father had given Him everything and that He had come from God and would return to God" that He wrapped a towel around His hips and began to wash the disciples' feet and to wipe their feet with the towel.

Let me ask you a question now. How many men do you know who are strong and stalwart and secure enough to serve their family like Christ served these disciples, His chosen family? Let me make it more personal: Do you serve your family, or do you make them serve you? Do you think you are a great dad or husband because you have exalted yourself to kingship in your family? According to the divine Word of God, our greatness comes from being a servant, not in being served.

> *The more lowly your service to others, the greater you are. To be the greatest, be a servant. But those who think themselves great shall be disappointed and humbled; and those who humble themselves shall be exalted (Matthew 23:11-12 TLB).*

I was at a party the other day where I heard one ill-advised husband say to his wife, "I'm the king in this house. Go get me some more goodies." Then he laughed and turned to me and said, "Ain't that right, preacher?"

You see, we men are so self-centered that we are very insecure with the idea of being a servant. It takes guts for a man to serve his wife or children, because those around him will say he is henpecked, and no man wants to be henpecked. But there is a difference between a man who is henpecked and one who is a servant. A husband who loves his wife so much that he has pushed self-love off the throne does everything in his power to see to the needs of his wife. He serves her, as a servant, willingly and graciously and happily because he loves her and not himself. But the man who is henpecked is a weak individual who allows his wife to bully him around and, of course, this is sickening.

The point that needs to be made as clear as possible is that the man who thinks he is great by being served by his family is out of line with the biblical concept of authority.

Jesus had all authority, and yet He humbled himself as a slave to men and even went so far as to actually die a criminal's death on a cruel cross.

> *Yet it was because of this that God raised him up to the heights of heaven and gave him a name which is above every other name (Philippians 2:9 TLB).*

The greatest husband and dad is the one who serves best and looks after every need and detail of his family. Thus he is in line with God's plan, and as a result will be exalted by God and his family to a place of honor to the glory of God, the greatest Father of all.

Most men are so afraid that they will end up making all the sacrifices and doing all the work. This fear leads them to doubt the work of God, and so they fail to follow through and get cold feet and go back to their old self-centered way, a way God never intended them to go. Jesus said, *"I am the Way—yes, and the Truth and the Life. No one can get to the Father except by means of me"* (John 14:6 TLB). You and I say with Philip, *"Sir, show us the Father and we will be satisfied"* (John 14:8 TLB). It is a man's nature to want proof, to be shown, to see and feel with his own senses. But if a man can't go it on faith, he cannot please God. It is not that God doesn't want us to have proof—there is plenty of it available for every man to see—but it is only in faith that a man is able to see it.

We are like Thomas, "the twin." We are his twin, for we want evidence. But Jesus said to Thomas, and He says to us, *"Put your finger into my hands. Put your hand into my side. Don't be faithless any longer. Believe!"* (John 20:27 TLB).

When we have tested these principles of Jesus, then our response will be like Thomas, too. "My Lord and my God!"

So I'm saying that we get to God and our inheritance by means of Jesus, for He is the Way, the Truth, and the Life. If Jesus is the Truth, then we had better pay attention, or else we will miss the abundant life God has prepared for us before we were ever born.

> *So overflowing is his kindness towards us that he took away all our sins through the blood of his Son, by whom we are saved; and he has showered down upon us the richness of his grace—for how well he understands us and knows what is best for us at all times (Ephesians 1:7-8 TLB).*

In other words, this principle of being a servant is given for our best interest as husbands and fathers, and if we believe it and allow Jesus to be Lord of our lives, then God will shower down all the riches of His grace.

All authority was given Jesus because He went to the cross and died a criminal's death. But we are the criminals in that we have made a gross violation of the law of God which says that we are to love our wives as Christ loved the church and gave Himself up for it. If you and I will go to the cross of Christ in faith and die of ourselves, then God will raise us up and will give us all authority even as He gave it to Christ.

Jesus asked His disciples, "Can you be baptized with the baptism with which I am baptized?" when they wanted to be elevated to a place of authority, and they said, "We can!" Although they did not know what was involved in this service of baptism, they were willing, but Jesus had to tell them, "Whoever wants to be greatest of all must be slave of all."

So if you are a slave in your own home, then you will be a happy slave, for you are imitating Christ. You are helping your household, you are different from other men, for you do not lord it over the family. We are either slaves to self and Satan or to the Savior. If we are slaves to ourselves, then we are most miserable and very confused, but if we are slaves to Jesus and to our homes, then we are celebrating with a party and feast that is attended by the angels and God Himself. Your home is a festive and glorious experience when your authority comes through a recognition of who you are, a child and heir of the Almighty Father through servitude.

> *Suddenly, the angel was joined by a vast host of others—the armies of heaven—praising God: "Glory to God in the highest heaven," they sang, "and peace on earth for all those pleasing him" (Luke 2:13-14 TLB).*

According to the angel's song, there is peace on earth and therefore within our hearts and homes when we please God.

> *You can never please God without faith, without depending on him. Anyone who wants to come to God must believe that there is a God and that he rewards those who sincerely look for him (Hebrews 11:6 TLB).*

"My Lord and my God," Thomas exclaimed when Jesus said, "Believe!" Hopefully and prayerfully, this will be your response as you read this—that you will say,

Okay, Lord, I believe. I'm going to trust that You know what You are asking, and I'm going to begin now dying to my selfish desires and begin serving my family lovingly and joyfully. Amen and amen.

In this chapter, we have tried to help you see more clearly your role of authority and how it comes about. You have rejected this authority because you have been unwilling to die to your ego, unwilling to be a servant to your Lord and your family. You have not realized the reward that comes to you when you humble yourself in the proper attitude to become to your wife what Christ became to the Church. When you come under new management, then your home comes under new management, and your family structure takes on a new form—a divine order which enables you to reap the glories God designed you to have.

In the next chapter, we will seek to answer your question, "Honey, what do you want me to do?" To answer that, your wife might say, "I want you to be what God intended you to be."

The first chapter of the Bible gets us straight on that point by telling us that we were made in God's image (Genesis 1:26). This image, or essence, is like God Himself. You have a mind with which to reason, a will with which to make decisions, and emotions with which to feel and express yourself. Knowing this about yourself, then you can understand that you can relate to God your Creator, Savior, Lord, and Guide. You can speak to Him and listen when He speaks to you. You are first of all the object of His infinite love, and you respond to that by loving Him back through others— your immediate family and the larger family of God.

By being obedient to God's way for your life, you can do your own thing in that context, for He is counting on you to live for Him in your small but significant spot. Where you fail, the Kingdom (Rule of God) fails. Where you do not let the light of God's Spirit shine, there will be darkness. Thus God needs you doing His thing, which involves much more than you are aware of at this time.

A man of God is not just the preacher. He is the man who is responsible to Christ and seeks to be in the place God has prescribed for him or ordered for him.

SEVEN

Wife and Death

K ing David provides another illustration of how our heroes operate. David was having trouble sleeping one afternoon and got up from his siesta to take a walk on the roof of the royal lodge. From this vantage point, he could look out over the city. *"He noticed a woman of unusual beauty taking her evening bath" (II Samuel 11:2 TLB)*. Another saint bit the dust. He indulged in reverie and his fantasy led him into an unrestrained extravaganza. He sent a messenger to find out who that gorgeous doll was. Even though she was the wife of Uriah, one of David's infantrymen, he sent for her. David was overcome by the beauty of Bathsheba. She went back home, and in time, when *"she found that he had gotten her pregnant she sent a message to inform him" (II Samuel 11:5 TLB)*.

In his palace, David panicked. He tried to cover up his sin and got deeper and deeper into trouble. His fleeting moment of fantasy turned into a nightmare for him, for the Lord was displeased. He sent the prophet Nathan to tell David the following story:

There were two men in a certain city, one very rich, owning many flocks of sheep and herds of goats; and the other very poor, owning nothing but a little lamb he had managed to buy. It was his children's pet and he fed it from his own plate and let it drink from his own cup; he cuddled it in his arms like a baby daughter. Recently a guest arrived at the home of the rich man. But instead of killing a lamb from his own flocks for food for the traveler, he took the poor man's lamb and roasted it and served it.

David was furious. "I swear by the living God," he vowed, "any man who would do a thing like that should be put to death; he shall repay four lambs to the poor man for the one he stole, and for having no pity" (II Samuel 12: 1-6 TLB).

Then Nathan came up with the clincher, "You are the man!"

God used Nathan the prophet as a vessel for the Holy Spirit to work in the heart of David. Hopefully, this book will have served the same purpose, that of being a vessel for the Holy Spirit to convict you of the fact that *you* are the man. You are the one who needs to change. It is my prayer that you will respond to the work of the Holy Spirit as did David when he prayed,

I admit my shameful deed—it haunts me day and night. It is against you and you alone I sinned, and did this terrible thing. You saw it all, and your sentence against me is just. Create in me a new, clean heart, O God, filled with clean thoughts and right desires.

96

Don't take your Holy Spirit from me. Restore to me again the joy of your salvation, and make me willing to obey you. Then I will teach your ways to other sinners, and they—guilty like me—will repent and return to you ... Oh, how I will praise you ... It is a broken spirit you want ... a broken and a contrite heart, O God, you will not ignore. (Psalm 51 TLB).

Here was King David, our hero, just like a member and elder of First Church, a connoisseur, a Little League coach, a member of the jet set—all these things, and yet here he was on his knees admitting what a sinner he was. This David, in all his splendor, was our hero. He might even have remained our hero if he had pulled off his caper with Bathsheba, but how can he be our hero while he admits that he is wrong? Why couldn't he have rationalized? He could have used the pressure of being in all those clubs, the pressure of being in war, the pressure of being home all day, the pressure of being a superstar. If David had been the man society would have him be, surely he could have blamed somebody or something for his folly and fantasy. But no, this guy had to be superhuman even in this denouncement. He confessed to the prophet Nathan, and the prophet replied,

"Yes, but the Lord has forgiven you, and you won't die for this sin. But you have given great opportunity to the enemies of the Lord to despise and blaspheme him, so your child shall die ... I vow that because of what you have done I will cause your own household to rebel against you" (II Samuel 12:13-14,11 TLB).

Even this great guy, this hero, had to reap what he sowed, but he did receive the forgiveness of God. He had fellowship with the Almighty, and he received the blessings of God.

When this David in his old age was relinquishing his kingdom, he said to his son, Solomon,

> Be strong then, show yourself a man, and do your duty to the Eternal your God, by living his life, by following his rules and orders and regulations and directions, as written in the law of Moses, so that, whatever you do and wherever you turn, you may have success, that the Eternal may fulfill his promise to me that if my children are careful how they live, living loyally under   his eye, with all their mind and ail their soul, I shall never lack a man upon the throne of Israel" (1 Kings 2:2-4 Moffatt).

King David was showing himself a man when he was on his knees saying, "Lord, I did it."

How about you? Why not go ahead and be a real man—confess your sin—get right with God—get on your knees and ask God to open your eyes, your heart, your will to be able to show yourself a man!

In much of what I have written, have you not seen yourself being rebellious toward your wife? Haven't you shown yourself as a rebel more than a man? Haven't you been so self-righteous that you stink? Hasn't your pride kept you from bowing before God and admitting how inadequately you have functioned as a husband and father? Hasn't your self-sufficiency kept you from being dependent upon God, saying to yourself, "Who needs God?" Haven't you been indifferent and inefficient in your role as husband and father?

This Holy Spirit that you and I and King David pray for is a treasure in us earthen vessels. But He, the Holy Spirit, cannot be released as long as He is trapped by our ego. If we pray for brokenness, then this Holy Spirit will provide us with adequate power to please God and function as true husbands and fathers.

When we men try to take things in our own hands, we really get God's world in a mess. My prayer is that God will help you overflow with joy in Him through the Holy Spirit's power within you.

It was the Holy Spirit of God that brought order out of chaos at creation, and He can do it now, beginning today, in your family. It was the Spirit of God who breathed life into man, and man became a living soul. It is that same Holy Spirit who operates today, and He can bring your soul and family back to life if you will simply open up and say:

Yes, Lord Jesus. I admit my nature of sin. Thank You for cleansing me and forgiving me my sins, and thank You now for coming into my heart and home. I'm asking You, Lord, to take up residence in my heart so I can be the head of my home.

God provides a kingdom to every man who marries, and he is responsible for the way he operates in that kingdom. If you have been operating your kingdom in the area of "self" domain, then your ego should be put to death (II Samuel 12:5 TLB).

How can a man die to self? It is not something a man does to himself—it is a matter of crucifixion. No man can crucify himself. What every man has to do to die of self-sufficiency and self-will and self-determination is to exercise faith in the work of Christ—simply to accept what Christ did for you on Calvary. When you believe, here is what happens:

> *For you have become a part of him, and so you died with him, so to speak, when he died; and now you share his new life, and shall rise as he did. Your old evil desires were nailed to the cross with him; that part of you that loves to sin was crushed and fatally wounded, so that your sin-loving body is no longer under sin's control, no longer needs to be a slave to sin; for when you are deadened to sin you are freed from all its allure and its power over you. And since your old sin-loving nature "died" with Christ, we know that you will share his new life ... So look upon your old sin nature as dead and unresponsive to sin, and instead be alive to God, alert to him, through Jesus Christ our Lord ...*
>
> *Do not let any part of your bodies become tools of wickedness, to be used for sinning; but give yourselves completely to God—every part of you—for you are back from death and you want to be tools in the hands of God, to be used for his good purposes (Romans 6:5-8;11,13 TLB).*

The chief purpose of man is to glorify God and enjoy Him forever.

> *God's glory is man made in his image, and man's glory is the woman (I Corinthians 11:7 TLB).*

What am I trying to say? I am saying that the solution to your home problem lies in the death of your self-image. That death comes about non-meritoriously by believing in Christ and the purpose of His death on the Cross.

> *For it is from God alone that you have your life through Christ Jesus. He showed us God's plan of salvation; he was the one who made us acceptable to God; he made us pure and holy and gave himself to purchase our salvation. As it says in the Scriptures, "If anyone is going to boast, let him boast only of what the Lord has done" (I Corinthians 1:30-31).*

There are many men who say, "I'm a self-made man." But if you are, then you are not in the image of God. You are out of fellowship and therefore out of line for all God has available for you. An inheritance comes only after death, and so until your old nature dies, you cannot have the spiritual promises of God.

> *For by the help of the eternal Holy Spirit, Christ willingly gave himself to God to die for our sins—he being perfect, without a single sin or fault. Christ came with this new agreement so that all who are invited may come and have forever all the wonder God has promised them (Hebrews 9:14-15 TLB).*

> *And so we should not be like cringing, fearful slaves, but we should behave like God's very own children, adopted into the bosom of his family, and*

calling to him, "Father, Father." For his Holy Spirit speaks to us deep in our hearts, and tells us that we really are God's children. And since we are his children, we will share his treasures—for all God gives to his Son Jesus is now ours too. But if we are to share his glory, we must also share his suffering (Romans 8:15-17 TLB).

But we need not panic at the suffering, for Christ says:

"Everything has been entrusted to me by my Father. Only the Father knows the Son, and the Father is known only by the Son and by those to whom the Son reveals him. Come to me and I will give you rest— all of you who work so hard beneath a heavy yoke. Wear my yoke—for it fits perfectly—and let me teach you; for I am gentle and humble, and you shall find rest for your souls; for I give you only light burdens" (Matthew 11:27-30 TLB).

Whenever you trust in the work of Christ on that cruel cross, then you share the treasures, and get what Christ got— priesthood, kingship, and prophetic powers. The prophet of old said,

For unto us a Child is born, unto us a Son is given; and the government shall be upon his shoulder. These will be his royal titles: "Wonderful," "Counselor," "The Mighty God," "The Everlasting Father," "The Prince of Peace" (Isaiah 9:6 TLB).

"In Christ" we share or participate as husbands and fathers in this royal role and responsibility, and we are given supernatural powers through the Holy Spirit to perform our duties.

> *"Watch now," the Lord of Hosts declares, "the day of judgment is coming, burning like a furnace. The proud and wicked will be burned up like straw; like a tree, they will be consumed—roots and all" (Malachi 4:1 TLB).*

> *For the time has come for judgment, and it must begin first among God's own children (I Peter 4:17 TLB).*

> *But for you who fear my name, the Sun of Righteousness will rise with healing in his wings. And you will go free, leaping with joy like calves let out to pasture ... See, I will send you another prophet like Elijah before the coming of the great and dreadful judgment day of God. His preaching will bring fathers and children together again, to be of one mind and heart, for they will know that if they do not repent, I will come and utterly destroy their land (Malachi 4:2-3, 5-6 TLB).*

John the Baptist was that prophet who came to set everything in order, but men then as now rejected the preaching of repentance and did not recognize John the Baptist as the forerunner of the Messiah. Repentance and pardon are prerequisites for a personal Pentecost and provisions for power in the Kingdom of God. When a man sees this and permits himself to be baptized by Jesus in the Holy Spirit, then he is qualified to receive and serve in the royal titles of Jesus.

When we men try, in our own power, to be the spiritual heads of our homes, we fall flat on our faces. It is *only* in the authority of the Holy Spirit that we men can adequately function as God ordered it. This is where that healing comes for the sickness of our society. Will you let it begin now in you by repenting and inviting Jesus to baptize you with His Holy Spirit? This simple invitation in faith will bring light and glory to your soul. Do it now.

> *His presence within us is God's guarantee that he really will give us all that he promised; and the Spirit's seal upon us means that God has already purchased us and that he guarantees to bring us to himself. This is just one more reason for us to praise our glorious God (Ephesians 1:14 TLB).*

When Jesus commanded Peter to take his gear and rig out where it was deeper to catch a kit of fish, Simon replied, *"Sir, we worked hard all last night and didn't catch a thing. But if you say so, we'll try again"* (Luke 5:5 TLB). This is no doubt most men's response when they are asked to give their marriage another go. They feel that they have worked at it without much success, so what's the use of trying again.

But when Peter, even reluctantly following the wishes of the Lord, did as He said, he found to his utter amazement an overflow of fish. This overflow, not of fish, but of love, is available for you and me also, if we will do as our Lord says and launch out into deeper waters of faith and obedience. Are you willing now to give your marriage another go, to really commit yourself to total involvement? If so, then the next few pages of this book will give you the answer to your question, "Honey, what should I do?"

The subject of family and marriage and the home is an awesome one. Since we are all human, and we all make mistakes, there is no man that I know of who is a living example of what a husband and father should be, but we do have some ideals and principles given to us in God's Word. And if we live according to these, we know one thing—that our marriage and family and social life and everything else will be happier and more joyous and more glorious.

Quite often my family gets in a discussion about something, and the other day we were discussing what each thought marriage was. One would make a comment and then another and then finally our nine-year-old daughter, Plythe, said, "Marriage is a matter of life and death." She had seen us in some crises, as all children do when parents have to work out difficulties and differences of opinion and she had felt the intensity of family relationships. Taking a cue from that, I have decided that in reality, marriage for you is a matter of "wife and death." You have a wife and life abundant when you die to yourself, because then your family comes alive.

> *And Jesus answered them saying, "The hour is come, that the Son of man should be glorified. Verily, verily, I say unto you, except a corn of wheat fall into the ground and die, it abideth alone: but if it die, it bringeth forth much fruit. He that loveth his life shall lose it; and he that hateth his life in this world shall keep it unto life eternal. If any man serve me, let him follow me; and where I am, there shall also my servant be: if any man serve me, him will my Father honour"* (John 12:23-26).

When Adam loved his wife, he was actually loving himself because she was part of him. She was created out of his rib. She was his indispensable helpmeet in the maintenance of the family.

> *And the Lord God caused a deep sleep to fall upon Adam, and he slept: and he took one of his ribs, and closed up the flesh instead thereof; And the rib, which the Lord God had taken from man, made he a woman, and brought her unto the man. And Adam said, This is now bone of my bones, and flesh of my flesh: she shall be called Woman, because she was taken out of Man. Therefore shall a man leave his father and his mother, and shall cleave unto his wife: and they shall be one flesh. And they were both naked, the man and his wife, and were not ashamed (Genesis 2: 21-25).*

This established a divine pattern, and I believe that this pattern is to be followed in God's order, for there is a right woman for every man, with the exception of rare cases of celibacy. And when these two opposite halves come together, they make a whole, they make a completion. They make life as God intended it to be in marriage. And this is God's plan, but men and women both have neglected and failed to understand and live according to His plan. As a result, we have a lot of marriages that are not established in the way God wanted them to be, but in a way that society dictates.

For example, I knew a young couple (she was nineteen and he was twenty) who had been married for about five years and already they were having serious problems. I asked them why they got married and this was their story:

One day after school, they had a brainstorm and decided to run away. Without thinking it through, they started out hitch-hiking along the Ohio road to Cincinnati. They were overtaken by darkness and spent the night in an old abandoned barn. The next day they began walking along the road, and as God would have it, they were picked up by a car driven by an attorney. The lawyer found out that they were running away from home, so he talked them into returning home and bought their bus fare back to their hometown. Because of the pressure of society, the parents panicked and insisted that they get married, feeling sure they had engaged in sexual activity through the night. They were afraid the girl was pregnant (although no sex activity had taken place). So here was a couple, married while they were children, with no understanding of what marriage was all about and certainly unaware of God's divine plan.

God's plans have been fouled up so badly that in our present day society a large number of marriages end in divorce or separation or become wretched in their relationships because the partners did not ask for God's direction in the selection of a life mate. Men were not patient enough to wait for the one God had provided for them, or trust God's wisdom and plan in the matter.

There are a lot of reasons that men get married, and many of those reasons are wrong reasons. If a young man is not aware that God has for him the right one—the right mate— he will get married outside of God's plan and will have to suffer the consequences of it. Let me enumerate a few of those reasons:

You may get married for "security reasons." You may want a mother—you may want to be loved and babied. You may want someone to make decisions for you and to care for you.

You may get married out of pure selfishness. You may want a slave—a live-in maid—someone to do all of your housekeeping, pick up your clothes, cook for you—that sort of thing.

You may get married because you want a beauty queen you can show off, take around and display like you would your new car. This is an extension of self-love. This beauty queen is a reflection on a man and his ego.

You may get married out of lust, to satisfy your sex drive. You may even get married because you feel guilty and because you've had premarital sex. You feel guilty and trapped and feel you have to get married.

I talked with a young man, married for five years, who said he got married because he and his wife had had premarital sex. She thought she was pregnant, told her parents, and he felt pressured into marrying her. In the meantime, he was unhappy and had committed adultery with another womarn and was now in serious trouble with his emotions and inability to cope. I talked with the wife and she was a bundle of nerves, full of guilt, and terribly insecure for fear her husband did not love her. Because marriage is based on purity, this marriage will continue to be in trouble or end in divorce, unless both parties confess before God their sin and re-establish the relationship on honesty and purity. *"And the man and his wife were both naked, and were not ashamed" (Genesis 2:25).*

You may get married out of pride. You may get married because all of your buddies are getting married, and you don't want anyone to think you are one of those "funny boys."

You may get married out of rebellion. You've had a girl friend—you've been sweet on each other. She rejects you, and you say, "I'll show her." And you go out and marry the first girl that says yes. That shows your old girl that nobody rejects you. Sad to say, this often happens.

When I was in college, I had a friend who was in love with a very sweet young thing back in his hometown. He received word from her that she was going to marry another man. This was such a shock to him that out of rebellion, he asked a girl he had dated a few times to marry him, and she said yes. Naturally, the marriage fell apart after a few months. The girl realized her mistake, went back home, and they were divorced—all because the marriage was based on a false premise.

You may get married out of fear. You may be afraid of being alone or afraid of criticism or ridicule, or of not being loved or of what people think. You may even be afraid of your own feelings.

You may get married out of self-pity. Poor me, nobody cares for me, so I'm just going to get married. You're really in trouble!

A lot of marriages are in a lot of trouble because they were established for wrong reasons.

There is a right reason for men to get married and that's love, but you may get married for the right reason, but the wrong attitude. In other words, you might be in trouble because you have not been taught the divine order and the purpose and meaning of wedlock.

Even if you marry in love and believe that God was a part of your coming together, you may be asking, after several years of marriage, "God, why did You give me this one? Out of all the world, why did You give me this one?" That displays the wrong attitude.

You have not fully understood that marriage is a union. It is a coming together of two opposites. You keep saying, "My wife isn't like me." Of course, she isn't like you. God never intended her to be. She is a helper, complementary to you. Someone who would take up the slack where you lack. Your wife doesn't compete with you—she complements you. You say, "I could have married any girl I wanted." Did, you realize that God picked out the girl you now have, so that she could mature you?

So we read in God's Word, and we establish now what we are supposed to be seeing here.

For since a man and his wife are now one, a man is really doing himself a favor and loving himself when he loves his wife (Ephesians 5:28 TLB).

Now let me give you a positive principle here. The more sacrificially you love your wife, the more respectfully your wife will respond to you in every category of life.

Now here is the negative to that principle. If you withhold love from your wife by withholding attention, compliments, understanding, appreciation, then you're making a big mistake. Because your wife is you, then when you neglect her, you are actually neglecting yourself. When you are unfaithful to your wife, you are actually deceiving yourself. When you are over-critical of your wife in order to build up yourself, then you are being dishonest with yourself and hurting yourself.

Man, you can save your marriage, because you really are the savior of the home. You can save the family by dying to yourself. You can save your home by dying to self-interest, self-righteousness, and self-gratification. These are dissolved when you give way to Christ as the Captain of your soul. When you decide to let Christ save your life and save you from yourself, then you are being prepared to be the best kind of husband and the best kind of father. For only then can you be truly sacrificial in your love, as Christ loved the Church and gave himself for it.

EIGHT

Avenues To Heavenly Harmony at Home

Jesus Christ, who was eternal God, became involved with His family. In John 1:14 we read, "And the Word was made flesh, and dwelt among us, (and we beheld his glory, the glory as of the only begotten of the Father,) full of grace and truth." He became involved in the details of life, and therefore God set Him up as the High Priest. His authority came from the fact that He became involved. You may want to be a priest in your home without being involved, but that is impossible. You *have* to be involved in the details of your wife and family. You must be ready to listen to your wife and to get involved with the details.

My wife went out and bought a couple of dresses. I said, "Wonderful!" I had been after her for years to do something on her own. I was so happy about that. It dawned on me later that the reason that I was so happy about her going out and buying those dresses was because I didn't have to go help her pick them out and become involved in the details of it.

I have to confess here that I'm really excited when my wife goes out to circle meetings on Monday nights, because then I can watch the NFL Monday night football game, prop up my feet, eat peanuts, munch on goodies and generally mess up. I don't have to listen to her. I'm glad, because I don't want to be involved in the things that she has to say and the problems that she has been presented with. I just want to ignore them. I just want to sit and enjoy something that I like to do—because I am selfish.

Men, we feel like we are too good to become involved in the needs of our wife or our children. But we need to take time to hear them out, to help them to discuss and work through the problems they have. Oh yes, you'll get involved with your neighbor's building program, or involved with another man's wife, or involved in some sports activity, or involved in your business. But you'll neglect the greatest business on earth—that of building a spiritual foundation for your own home. Your failure to function as priest in your home contributes to the chaos and makes life miserable for each member of the family.

The role of the husband and father as priest is truly a sacred gift of God to man. If you rebel against that responsibility, if you do not receive that gift, then God cannot bless you. You will not have the glory God intends for you. And as a result, your home will continue to dwell in "tents of turmoil." No peace can come to your household apart from the peace that Christ gives when He is accepted as a man's High Priest, and man becomes the priest of his family.

The one big thing that men want, but are failing to get, is peace in the home, never realizing that peace comes not from appeasement but from his "priesthood."

Jesus Christ became involved in the needs of mankind; so much so, that he suffered and died for man. He sacrificed Himself. He Gave Himself. Jesus had the freedom and the power to lay down His life, and He chose to do it. Because Jesus Christ became involved, He received the glory, the authority, the majesty, the priesthood and the lordship. And therefore, He provided the peace. This principle is true for each of the divine institutions—nation, family, and marriage—but is particularly appropriate for the institution of the family.

God the Father, throughout all eternity, had an only begotten Son. But the Father-heart of God desired a family. Be careful to see that the Fatherhood of God is rooted, not in the creation of Adam, but rather in the Redemption by His only begotten Son. Because "in Adam," all have sinned and come short of the glory of God. The miracle of all miracles was the sacrificial death of Christ. For in that Cross, God's mightiest act was to translate man "in Adam" to man "in Christ" (I Corinthians 15:45-47). (This is not automatic, but by your faith.)

Jesus is the "last Adam," and as such He is the sum total of humanity, dying on the Cross to satisfy the righteousness and Justice of God. Jesus picked up the tab for all our sin. Jesus is also the "second Man," and as such He became the head of a new race, and God put us in that seed to redeem us for the purpose of glory. Men, we are missing the glory of God when we do not believe God's Holy Word and trust His work. The beautiful eighth chapter of Romans points this out so clearly.

Here is what has happened "in Christ." The only begotten Son, as described in the incarnation of John 1:14, becomes the first begotten Son of a new race in Romans 8:29, for the purpose of the peace in Ephesians 2:13-19, the purpose of the glory in Romans 8:21-30, and the purpose of the posterity in Romans 8:15-16, and all this leads to priesthood in Hebrews 2:9-3:12.

My conclusion of the matter then of the work of Christ as High Priest is the principle of involvement through which men, as husbands and fathers, must go in order to have peace in their homes. Therefore, the Fatherhood of God is not independent of His only begotten Son, and neither is it independent of the existence of parents. My son's opportunity to experience the Fatherhood of God comes through me, his earthly Father. I am not only the representative of God the Creator, to whom the descendants owe their life, but I am also a link in the historical line of the people of God.

Thus, the father bears a sacred office. He takes God's place and has no authority or right, except that which is given him by God. God has given man freedom to lay down his life, and that power comes from being "in Christ."

When a man does as Jesus did—puts the death principle to work, dies to self, and allows the Holy Spirit to control his soul—he becomes a new man and puts the resurrection principle to work in his life.

The apostle Paul discusses this principle in Ephesians 2:13-19:

But now in Christ Jesus ye who sometimes were far off are made nigh by the blood of Christ. For he is our peace, who hath made both one; and hath broken down the middle wall of partition between us; Having abolished in his flesh the enmity, even the law of commandments contained in ordinances; for to make in himself of twain one new man, so making peace; And that he might reconcile both unto God in one body by the cross, having slain the enmity thereby; And came and preached peace to you which were afar off, and to them that were nigh. For through him we both have access by one Spirit unto the Father. Now therefore ye are no more strangers and foreigners, but fellow-citizens with the saints and of the household of God.

The above Scripture tells us how Christ reconciled the Jews and Gentiles to each other and man to God, which brought peace. Christ was able to do this by dying on the Cross.

Now there is in your home a wall that has been built up between you and your wife, you and your children, the sons and daughters, brothers and sisters. You have all become strangers and foreigners in your own household. Why? Because you have not been "in Christ" using that "work" that Christ performed on Calvary.

When you, by faith, enter into Christ, then the character of Christ begins to form in you, and you begin to produce the first true love, a love so great that you, the head of the home, lay down your life for your family.

You become priest of your family when you are abiding "in Christ," and then the warmth of Christ's love flows through you and begins to open gates in that icy wall that has come between you and your family, thus bringing about joyous reconciliation, a peace that passes understanding, a legacy without bounds, a glory full of grace and truth. This is what you want, but you have either not been informed that this is "the way," or you have been too stubborn to try it.

Thus, being the priest in your home simply means being "in Christ," allowing Him to control your life in every phase and category—to provide a spiritual atmosphere of love and truth and openness to God and each other. Because you, the head of the home, are the initiator of love, then the other members respond happily to your approachableness, and this makes for a godly home, one that God honors and blesses.

"Preacher, if I had just known this when I was a young man, I could have done something about it. My children are all grown now, and it's too late for me to change," said one man after being exposed to this principle of priesthood.

"My mistakes have caused all this family turmoil," confessed one father after a period of consultation. "But what do I do now? It's all water over the dam, and I feel like it's too late for me to do anything now."

Men in their middle or late years of marriage find it difficult to see where these concepts will be of any help to their marriage, since it is about fmished. However, it is in these golden years of wedlock that men could really do themselves a favor and really enjoy being married. Don't let your age or the length of time you've been married confuse you into believing it is too late. Many games are won in the last inning or quarter or minutes, and you can still be a winner in your marriage.

"My wife has a problem," said a middle-aged man while I was talking with him. "She tells me the same things over and over again—maybe *hundreds* of times. What should I do?"

"What do you mean?" I questioned him.

"Well, I mean," he drawled, "she says the same things to me over and over, so I just pretend like I don't hear it and let her rattle on. I think she's losing her mind. Maybe I need to let her see a psychiatrist or something."

I took a deep breath and thought, "Lord, help me know how to answer this question." As we talked, I was able to see why his wife kept on and on, repeating herself.

"Because you are not counseling your wife about her hangups and troubles," I said, "she feels that need to talk excessively. Since you don't hear her out, or you sit there without responding, she probably thinks you're a little peculiar, too. A man who listens to his wife tell the same thing over and over again as if it were being told for the first time must admit that he's not dealing with the problem."

"I just thought that was the way to handle it," he said.

"Why don't you start listening to her in a loving way?" I asked. "Why don't you talk back to her and express your views and say what's on your mind? Or why don't you say, 'Honey, you've told me that before, remember?'"

"She's always gotten angry before when I told her that," he said. "I can't ever win. She always cries or pouts or shouts when I try to tell her something, so I've just learned to keep my mouth closed and let her rattle on."

"When you don't relate and react to what she says to you, no wonder she gets upset. She's frustrated. The next time she tells you a story or covers the same ground, repeat what she said and then ask her if that's what she said. Ask her what she means. Ask her how she feels about the incident with the child, or the neighbor, or whatever. Take this opportunity to help her see what's bugging her. Deal with it as sweetly as you can. In this way, you become her priest— giving her a chance to let off steam or get out her animosities or bitterness or fears or hurts."

"If I did that, I wouldn't have time to watch my television or read my paper. Besides, she does that all day long on the phone to her friends. Why should I have to be bothered with it?" he asked.

"You don't have to be, Mr. White," I answered, "unless you want her to pay a good portion of your salary for a psychiatrist or unless you want her to keep on just like she is. Really though, the reason should be simply because this is God's Way. You are *supposed* to be her priest."

"Are you trying to tell me that by my doing some of these things you said that she will change?" he asked in a surprised tone.

"Yes sir," I answered. "Would you pray with me right now, Mr. White, and ask the Spirit of God to show you how to be more loving and kind to your wife? To thank God for removing the resentment you have when you have to spend a little of yourself on your mate? To thank God for giving her to you and for forgiving you for not assuming your role as spiritual head of your home?"

We prayed that day, and since then, a transformation has taken place in that home. They are now like two newlyweds—always together. The man's devotion to his wife has caused a new surge of respect and saneness to that simple and sweet home. The married children are now overjoyed to have them in their homes, and the father has found a new place of honor in the eyes of his children and wife. I saw this man not long ago, and he put his arm around me and said, "Pastor, I've never been happier in my life since I've been showing more attention and love to my wife. I used to think it was so important to read the newspaper and find out what's going on in this world. Now I see it's more important to see what's going on in my family. I realize how close I came to losing my wife—and, frankly, there were times when I secretly wished I would lose her. But now I can see it was all my fault. God has been mighty good to me, and I'm praising His name every day for forgiving me and giving me another chance. Preacher, I've been telling men my age, 'It's never too late to change.' I've been telling them what you told me. Most of them think I'm a religious nut, a fool. But if that's what I am, then, I'm the happiest fool in the world. I was miserable before and seldom had a happy moment. Now I'm joyous with life—especially my home."

The model prayer of Matthew 6:9-13 offers a beautiful example of "Mr. Wonderful," or Father-King. It begins, "Our Father," and quickly moves to "thy Kingdom come." When a man comes in line with God's order, he then, by inheritance, becomes a father-king. If Christ is King, in your soul, then you are king in your home. When Christ rules you, then you can rule your wife and children.

There is a danger here, for many men forget that their kingship is a birthright and end up abusing it. You can be one of three kinds of kings—a wicked king, a righteous king, or an indifferent king. You can deliberately choose to be a tyrant, or you can be a good provider, or you can dwindle away your kingship in sloppy or indifferent decisions.

To see yourself as a good king means that you treat your wife like a queen and your child like a princess or prince. God offers us provisions, pardon, and protection when we see Him as Sovereign Father-King in the Lord's Prayer. And so it is with a man who comes in line with the divine order, for God has given him that "wonderful" position.

This kingship, then, is quite a responsibility, but with every responsibility comes a reward, so the man who delivers the goods in this role as king becomes "Mr. Wonderful" in the eyes of his kingdom. That's a rich reward, too good to pass up, and yet you may be missing out.

Be aggressive in the love-making department. I know some men who are waiting around for their wives to take the initiative in the sex act. And they'll probably wait for a long time, because God never intended it to be that way. God is the aggressor in the love-making to mankind. He took the initiative, and we men have that responsibility, too. We are supposed to be the aggressors.

When it comes to the subject of love-making, you have been bombarded by society and the playboy philosophy so hard that you are no doubt confused. You may have the idea that your wife is like your golf bag, there for you to use when you get the urge, and then to be stuck in the closet when you're through, to be there when you're ready again. But you are mistaken.

One woman told me, "My husband can find more to read in one newspaper than anyone else in the world. He can spend hours reading the paper while I rake the yard, clean the house, and cook—without even knowing I am around. Then when he finishes reading the paper, he comes over and wants to make love to me. I just can't respond, because it makes my blood boil. Then he says, 'Honey, is anything wrong?' I've told him hundreds of times that I can't get excited by being pinched, pawed, and patted—especially when he has done 'nothing' to show his love."

"Your husband is not one of a kind," I acknowledged. "In fact, most men are that way." No wonder some women feel the need to leave home—because there is nothing much to leave.

Jesus Christ is the best friend we will ever have, for He pointed out the value of truth, the truth that sets us free. Too long we men have been deceived by our own choice to serve ourselves rather than live for our Lord Jesus. As a prophet "in Christ," you are set free to see how cruel and evil you have been to your wife and family. It will cause you to repent and come into His way and will. When you do this, your marriage will come back from the dead, and new visions of hope and sounds of love and feelings of joy and tastes of honesty and smells of goodness will come into your home.

When you begin walking in God's way, your wife will become a follower, and she will begin to tag along behind, because women are made by God to be that way. When you deny yourself and go the second mile with the proper attitude, your wife will honor and respect you and love you in subjection as unto the Lord.

Now I want to go back to that illustration that I used earlier of the couple I saw at the grocery store, the man who had the bad attitude. Let's turn that around and say he understood himself to be a prophet of his home and understood the principle of the second mile that God teaches us through His Word. That man could have said, "Sweetheart, here, let me push the cart; let me help you out a little bit." That evening the wife might have said something like, "Here, sugar, you sit right down here in your nice soft easy chair and watch that basketball game." Then she would swish off and in a minute return with his favorite beverage and with a gentle, sweet peck on the cheek say, "Darling, if you need anything, just let me know."

Then shortly the husband would say, "Here, honey, let me help you put the children to bed." After helping her with the children, he would take her by the hand. They would go to the den and talk over the day's activities, sharing their day, their thoughts, their desires, their hopes, and their dreams. Later that night, his wife would respond to his love and thoughtfulness in an adequate way. When you take the initiative in showing love throughout the day, your wife is made by God to respond to that love.

God is the one who invented sex, and He's been around much longer than the philosophy of free love. When God brought Eve to Adam, and he saw her for the first time, his eyes bugged out, and he exclaimed, "At last, this is it!" Adam saw that God had designed him for giving and Eve for receiving—perfect fit!

This was God's doing, and God has designed for every man a right woman for a wife—perfectly fit for him physically, emotionally, intellectually, spiritually.

When you married, when you received the girl God gave you, there was no need to try her out for size, God doesn't make mistakes. Man is the one who fouls things up.

It is God's plan that you marry the one woman He has chosen for you and that you find in her alone the fulfillment of your sex drives within the bounds of the divine institution of marriage. God has made you the pursuer, and once you have captured her heart, the courtship continues to sail on the sea of matrimony. Never forget that your wife is made differently from you, and her physiological needs are not as demanding as yours. Therefore, you have the major responsibility in creating the proper atmospheric conditions to provide the gentle breeze and to set the sails in the proper attitude to move the courtship into the haven for which the heart of a woman truly longs.

You cannot have a knock-down-drag-out fight or be in contention or wrapped up in the television and then expect your wife to respond to you sexually. You cannot go on letting her make all the decisions, pay the bills, take care of the house and yard, tend to all the correspondence, do all the shopping, take care of the discipline of the children, and then expect her to get excited when you touch her and kiss her and start playing around.

Your wife is not aroused in the same way you are. She has to feel protected, cared for, understood—not necessarily fondled—and that is where you fumble and falter.

I talk with couple after couple who can't seem to work out their sex problem because the man is so childish and immature on the subject.

"It burns me up," said one man, "when my wife rejects me. She is my wife, and I have a right to her body, and if she turns me off, I get furious." (See 1 Corinthians 7:4.)

"Yes, I know," I replied, "but don't you reject her first?"

"Heck no," he exclaimed. "I'm always ready for sex, and she can tell you that."

"I'm sure she can," I replied, "but do you know why your wife rejects you in the bed?"

"No," he said, "unless she's mad at me for something."

"Yes, and also because you have rejected her in the head," I said. "I'll give you a secret that will usually prepare your wife for sex activity—if you will listen," I stated.

His eyes got big, and a grin came upon his tired face, and he said, "I'm listening, I'm listening!"

"The secret is in talking with your wife," I told him, watching the smile fall from his face and his brow begin to wrinkle.

"I'm sorry," he queried, "I thought I heard you say *talking*."

"Yes, sir," I replied. "It is in talking with your wife that you let her take off your clothes, so to speak. She 'takes off' your shirt of self-righteousness, your pants of self-sufficiency, your undershorts of self-pity. This is what stimulates her sexually. When she is allowed to come into your intimate world of selfhood—what you normally cover from the world—it makes her responsive to you. Then she is ready to open up to you—to let you come into *her* world—physically, emotionally sexually, whatever. Do you understand what I am saying?"

"Preacher," he said, "I've heard a lot of stuff about how to make out with your wife, but I've never heard this before. You mean when I come home from work and I talk with Marie and tell her about my day or my thoughts or my ideas that she is gonna get excited?"

"That will be a beginning," I answered.

"I sure thought there was more to it than just talking," he replied, scratching his head.

"Well, it has to do with the attitudes," I said. "If you show an attitude of humility, an attitude of gratitude for her as a wife or person, an attitude of interest in what she is experiencing, an attitude of helpfulness in the home life, an attitude of attention toward her and the children, then you will be communicating to her vibrations of love that will truly excite and stimulate her in every way."

"Well I'll be darned!" he exclaimed. "You mean if I wouldn't reach for the paper or the television button, but would reach instead for my wife's needs, then I'd get good news and turn her on instead of off?" he asked.

"That's a good way of putting it," I answered.

This is the way a man does himself a favor by loving his wife as Christ loved the Church and gave Himself for it.

Very few men want to "spend" themselves on their wives. They want to get by with as little as they can, and so they have a cheap marriage. This is what is wrong with the playboy philosophy. When a man has cheap experiences with his wife or with other women, he never gets satisfied. He thinks he is being cheated by his wife or the other women he uses, not realizing that he is cheating himself. When a man gives totally of self (ego) to his wife, true satisfaction in sex and in every phase of life comes as a result. It is a risk, but it must be taken if you want to experience more of what God intended in marriage.

A wife is aroused sexually when her husband allows her to undress him—not physically, but within. When a man gives himself to his wife, letting her expose his thoughts, his emotions, his self-will, then she has no difficulty giving herself to him sexually. If men could understand that love is inviting your wife into your world, allowing her to see you, to disrobe you, to pull down your self-righteousness, self-sufficiency, selfhood, self-idolatry, and self-determination, then they would get the proper response from their wives.

Men wrap themselves up from their wives by being egotistic, by not sharing their problems, their hang-ups, their desires, their antagonisms, their dreams with their wives. When you withhold this from your wife, you reject her. So it is little wonder that she then rejects you sexually when you begin trying to take off her clothes. In other words, the sexual foreplay of a woman is a soul activity in which she is allowed the privilege of seeing your exposed ego. When this intimacy of soul is denied a wife, she denies her husband the sex activity or intimacy of her body. Or else she lets you use her body without responding with her feelings. Then she feels guilt— put there by you when you claim she is frigid.

Men are to love their wives as Christ loved the Church and gave Himself (ego) for it. Jesus, through communication of His mind, exposed Himself on the cross of Calvary—nude before all mankind—to show His love for His bride, the Church. This was a total commitment of Himself—nothing left on—totally exposed—totally spent for love.

When we men can catch this sweet mystery of love, then we will experience more of the ecstasy of love and less of the agony of life and wife. *"Now although the man and his wife were both naked, neither of them was embarrassed or ashamed" (Genesis 2:25 TLB).* When your marriage is based upon honesty and purity and fidelity in Christ, then you experience this sweet innocence that allows you to trust, give, forgive, and give thanks.

One young couple, married about five years, have quite a time of it because when he begins making advances toward her sexually, she turns him off. He gets angry and bounds out of the bedroom, and here they go again. Instead of listening to her, talking with her about the problem, he ignores it until the next time he gets the biological urge, and it's the same thing all over again. All he needs to do is to discuss it with her, and she could tell him what excites her, but he is too stubborn, and so he's missing out on what God has for him in sex because he won't take time to learn and listen.

I talked with another couple and learned that the wife had experienced only a few sexual climaxes in the five years of their marriage. Her husband was too slow to catch on and too selfish to realize the damage he was doing to his lovely wife. Every night she dreaded going to bed, because she knew the hurt she would have to go through in being made to feel like a heel in not getting any sexual relief. So she would make all kinds of excuses about being too tired, or wanting to stay up longer, or whatever. I asked her why she did not talk with him about it and she said, "I don't want to hurt his ego, because he thinks he's such a great lover."

Now it doesn't take too much intelligence to realize that your wife is not responding sexually like she should, so all you have to do is open up and admit that you have made some mistakes, that you are doing something wrong, and that *you* need help.

This is a problem area in your homes, all because you have not been aggressive enough to find out how to handle the problem. Instead, you pout, you rebel, you look elsewhere, you get angry, you take advantage, you take for granted. You do everything but the one thing you and you alone can do, and that is to go find help—or be man enough to open up to your wife about the problem and patient enough to work out the hang-ups you have caused and be kind enough to admit it is your fault.

God created sex, and it is good, but you have made it ugly by your ugly attitude, your unwillingness to let it be the response of a loving wife to a loving husband who becomes involved in the details of his home life, who studies his wife and knows her ultimate needs, who takes hold of the family affairs and sees to it that the bills are paid and decisions are made, who is understanding, and who disciplines the children and teaches them God's love by the way he shows love to his wife in the home.

As a good king then, you must be the perseverer in lovemaking, not the perverter of love-making. Hang in there regardless of the counter-influences, opposition, and discouragement. Otherwise, you will pervert the whole plan of God in sex and come out a wretched king with a kingdom in ruins.

As a good king, it is also your responsibility to initiate in the reconciliation and pardon department. Don't wait around for your wife to say, "I'm sorry." You initiate it with those six very important words, "I was wrong. I am sorry." Your attitude might be, "But I'm never wrong!" But God is our King and even though He was definitely not wrong, He initiated our reconciliation to Him by sending the Word, Jesus.

Long ago, even before he made the world, God chose us to be his very own, through what Christ would do for us; he decided then to make us holy in his eyes, without a single fault—we who stand before him covered with his love (Ephesians 1:4 TLB).

This kind of king is secure and offers pardon and protection to his wife. He sees in her no fault because he loves her so deeply, as Christ loved His bride, the Church. *"If a king is kind, honest and fair, his kingdom stands secure"* *(Proverbs 20:28 TLB)*. With a love and faith like this, your home is on the rock and *"all the powers of hell shall not prevail against it"* *(Matthew 16:18 TLB)*.

NINE

More Paths To Peace

One of the most important functions of a family is protection. *"Don't bring us into temptation, but deliver us from the Evil One" (Matthew 6:13 TLB)*. Because this is one of the requests that Jesus taught His disciples to make to their Father-King, then it seems to me of major importance for us earthly fathers. I believe this is what Paul had in mind when he wrote:

> *"And you husbands must be loving and kind to your wives and not bitter against them, nor harsh" (Colossians 3:19 TLB)*.

And again:

> *"Don't keep on scolding and nagging your children, making them angry and resentful" (Ephesians 6:4 TLB)*.

It is a King's love that protects (covers) His Kingdom and keeps the Evil One from attacking with his weapons of anger, bitterness, and resentfulness that are so ever-present around our kingdoms. This "love" that protects a man's family is the "better way" of I Corinthians 13, and the weapons of Ephesians 6:10-18 are the panoply of a godly king.

We men are quite guilty of tempting our wives to bitterness and disrespect by our failure to take care of the finances. Many men are exposing their wives to the harrassment of the world because of the financial bind they are in. When there is a lack of love within a home, the void is often filled with material objects, which are costly. The financial bind caused by providing the substitute of stuff for love often requires that the wife go outside the home to work.

Now, I am not so naive as to say all working mothers or wives are doing so because there is a lack of love on the part of the husband. In the description of a truly good wife by King Lemuel in Proverbs 31:24, we find that *"She makes belted linen garments to sell to the merchants" (TLB).* Thus, there is a legitimate time for a wife to help with the family budget. However, if it causes the wife undue stress and strain or gives her an excuse to evade her responsibilities as a wife and mother, then careful consideration must be given to see the real problem. I am concerned about men who either force or allow their wives to work out of the cruelty of their selfish motivation to acquire more social prestige at the awful expense of their wives and children.

I realize there is no blanket solution to this satanic home-breaking device of materialism, but a man who is under the control of the Holy Spirit will be able to offer maximum protection of His light and guidance in this maze of materialism.

Not only is there the problem of men not making enough money to make ends meet, but the situation of men with adequate salaries, yet by default "passing the buck" to their wives to sweat out the bill-paying game. There are many arguments pro and con in this area of home life, and I do not presume to have the last word, but the best word is God's Word which teaches that husbands are heads of their wives (I Corinthians 11:3) and as such must offer them protection.

This area of finances is just one area where the man (king) would cover his wife from the pressure and responsibility of deciding who gets paid and where the money is coming from. This is not to say that she must have no dealings with the money, but she should not have the burden of deciding who is to be paid or earning the living.

Another area of protection that women need from their husbands is in social circumstances. Paying attention to your own wife in situations where other men are involved is healthy and wholesome. But when a husband allows his wife to be exposed to the maudlin and mauling males at a social gathering, a marriage can go sour. Parties are a part of the gregarious life of human beings, but if men are negligent in providing support for their wives in a time when their defenses may be down, it contributes to a bad scene. Too many homes are being broken by the careless attitude of husbands who allow their wives to be exposed to wanton men. If you do not protect your wife, no one else will.

A man's responsibility as father-king is best illustrated in the way of love as the apostle Paul was inspired of the Holy Spirit to write to the Corinthian church. In his analysis of love (charity), the Holy Spirit makes it clear that love offers *protection*. Paul, guided by the Holy Ghost, offers nine qualities of love (I Cor. 13:4-6) that a man can use.

When we ask you to love your wife as Christ loved the Church, we are asking you to be the following nine things: patient with your wife and family, kind, generous, humble, courteous, unselfish, good-tempered, blameless, and honest.

Now, let me illustrate how these qualities can be put to practical use. When you and your wife are socializing, it is a perfect opportunity to protect her by being courteous.

I was at a social event not too long ago in which several couples had been invited for a covered-dish dinner. As the couples came in, it was interesting to watch how they acted and interacted with each other. As we ate, I found myself asking other men's wives if I could get them more to drink or more rolls, and then it dawned on me that I was taking away the right and privilege of the husbands to do that for their *own* wives. When other wives would get ready to sit or stand, the men would be courteous to the other ladies by fixing their chairs or seeing to it that they had what they needed. As I thought about this later, I realized that each husband needs to be courteous and sweet and thoughtful with his own wife. As one wife put it, "I don't want my husband giving attention to other wives that should be given to me." When each husband pays attention to his own wife, there is a sweet protection that keeps a lot of wrong feelings from getting started among couples.

Before the evening was over, I saw husbands being unkind and selfish before their wives, and no doubt it took some time for these couples to get back into a right relationship.

Oddly enough, most men or women do not really know what is going on. All they know is that something is wrong, and so they don't know how to handle the situation. How easy it would be if each husband would protect his own wife—by being kind and considerate and unselfish toward her.

A man should know if it bothers his wife to dance with other men, and if it does, then he should offer her protection from these men who ask her to dance by saying, "I'm sorry, she is my date for the evening," or something that would let him know you're not going to let your wife dance with anyone other than you. This may seem like a very small thing, and most men and even some women may say, "Well, how trifling can you get?" But if we don't start getting at some of these problems in the "trifling way" (that's what courtesy is), then we are going to continue to have this wave of confusion among couples.

I hear men and women both say, "I don't want to say anything about my husband opening the car door for another woman—it's so insignificant." Or a husband will say, "It will make me look like a jealous husband if I don't let my wife dance with other men." He never realizes that if he would learn to dance and offer her protection and courtesy, then his wife would respond to him in loving him back.

When couples go out together, a wall builds up when the wife gets the feeling that she isn't very important. The husband who ignores his own wife or overlooks her needs really cuts and hurts his wife. She can hardly stand it.

I have learned that there are some wives who are not receiving love and attention from their own husbands, and so when some other man is courteous and thoughtful toward them, it opens up feelings that become misdirected. Before you know it, the situation has gotten out of hand.

Because many men fail in the responsibilty of giving their wives love and attention, their wives seek it from other men. These flirty women are that way because of their own husbands. Women who seek attention from other men create tension among couples in any group where husbands and wives are together. I am aware through counseling that wives whose husbands respond to the flirting of other women get quite upset. Most men feel that it is silly for their wives to get upset over such a little thing as that. When a man laughs and says to his wife, "Honey, that's so petty," it closes the door and causes her to begin building feelings of resentment toward her husband, because he has failed to protect her.

If you learn that it is bothering your wife when you pay attention to a flirty woman, then the courteous thing to do is listen to your wife and show her attention. Then love rebounds from her to you in a favorable way. After all, it is more important to impress your own wife than it is someone else's, and the rewards are far greater. All a man has to do is ignore the flirty woman, and she will move on, but most men don't do that because they enjoy the attention and feelings they are getting. This is being unkind, selfish, proud, and dishonest. All of which means a lack of love for your own wife and therefore a lack of protection for her. When a man says, "But, honey, you know I love you," and yet the wife picks up feelings that she is the one being ignored, she will believe her feelings before she believes what she hears her husband saying.

Protecting your wife takes on a different color when you are in public. It is one thing to show love to your wife behind closed doors and pulled blinds, and it is quite another thing to show your wife love in public. Both are necessary. There are so many little acts of kindness that go by the board that we men let slip, and as a result, have to reap the consequences. Men, believe me, it is the little things that eventually count. The big things, like providing money for the needs of daily living, are a breeze, but it is the words of praise that get golden results.

A word fitly spoken is like apples of gold in pictures of silver (Proverbs 25:11).

It is these words of praise that protect a man's wife from the world, because then the world knows how a man feels about his wife. It is much easier for a husband to criticize his wife than it is to build her up. Many men are afraid to let other men know how they love their wives. It is hard enough for a husband to praise his wife in private, much more in public. But if men only knew how wonderful and lovely it makes a woman feel for her husband to stand up for her in public and praise her in public, he would do it continuously. It would truly build the relationship and make it strong and fortified.

We need to understand that marriage is more than a contract, it is a relationship. And that relationship is kept alive by our kindness and courtesy as well as our openness in conversation. Why is it so hard for a man to be kind to his wife? I believe the reason is because he is *afraid*. He is afraid of what other people will think, or he's afraid his wife will take advantage of him. What he doesn't know is that he would reap kindness and respect and peace from all who see and know, especially from his own wife. Fear is a tormenting spirit, and that spirit is cast out in perfect (mature) love.

> *There is no fear in love; but perfect love casteth out fear: because fear hath torment. He that feareth is not made perfect in love (I John 4:18).*

In other words, when a man is courteous, patient, humble, and good-tempered, then he is showing real love.

We are talking about very subtle ways that you as a husband can give your wife protection. It is a man's selfishness that dulls the joy of family living. We really need to check our motivation—why we do what we do. A good example of what I'm talking about happened to me just recently. I thought I was preparing my wife's breakfast for her one Saturday because I wanted to show her love. So I got up and put on the griddle and cooked sausage and bacon and pancakes and had the coffee all perked and went in and kissed my wife and told her that breakfast was ready. When she came out, she looked at the table and noticed that there was no orange juice, and so she said, "I'll make a pitcher of orange juice." I got angry and exclaimed, "By the time you do that, your pancakes will be cold!" She answered, "Well, Page, are you more concerned about cold pancakes or about me?"

Then I realized that all the effort I had exerted was not for Patti, but for my own ego—which is the way I do so many things. That was a lesson for me. I was angry because Patti had not received what I "thought" was a labor of love, and so I reacted in a selfish manner of anger and self-pity. You say, "That sure is a little thing," and you are right.

Courtesy is love in the trifles. When a man puts a razor to his beard every morning for a week, it becomes quite dull for shaving. Then, when he replaces that blade, he is made aware of what a difference it is to have a nice, clean, smooth shave. What I am saying, men, is that these little acts of kindness and courtesy are ways of keeping the blade sharp, so to speak, and doing yourself a favor—keeping a smooth and gentle and sweet home where peace and prosperity rule.

When you and I take God's Word seriously, believe it and live by it, then we are surrounded by His love, and our homes are protected from the evil one. What Satan wants is to confuse and mix up the family so that it loses its effectiveness. If Satan can get the home, he's well on his way to messing up God's good and perfect will. And we let the devil do it, men, by not standing on the Word (trusting God).

If God tells us that love does not seek its own way, then why are we so headstrong on getting our own way? If the Bible teaches that love is humble, then why are we so boastful? If the Spirit of God makes it known unto us that love is being good-tempered, then why are we so ill-tempered? What it all boils down to is that we men are not willing to admit that we are selfish and that we are disobeying the Word of God and therefore destroying the homes that God Himself has established.

Protection for our homes comes when we obey God's will and love the nine ways listed, not just to the people on the job, but to the people in your *own home*. If charity begins at home, then let it be real charity—not just a man giving his paycheck to his wife to deposit in the bank. Instead, love is a man giving his wife loyalty—no matter what the cost—

believing in her, always expecting the best of her, and always standing his ground in defending her.

> *If you love someone you will be loyal to him no matter what the cost. You will always believe in him, always expect the best of him, and always stand your ground in defending him (I Corinthians 13:7 TLB).*

A true king, a good king, is one who sees to it that his wife has all the provisions for life, for joy, for peace, for health, and for protection from Satan and his world. That, of course, is a tall order that cannot possibly be delivered apart from Christ as King in your life. If Christ is ruler of your soul, then you can be ruler of your home.

God has delegated to you the authority and kingship. The way the home goes is the way you make it go or the way you let it go. Therefore, if there is any trouble at all within your kingdom, then you are responsible for seeing that it gets worked out. You should handle the issues even if it means the two of you going to someone for counsel. What you may feel is nothing serious could be a very serious problem, and you're just not facing it. Most of us men feel that if there isn't too much static, all is well on the home front. Or you may think, why stir up the water if the wife isn't taking issue or if she isn't too angry. But that is the nature of a woman to let things build up until she explodes.

Men say, "My wife gets on one of those rages every few years, and we've been doing all that for all our married life."

My comment is, "Why don't we men try to find out what's causing the trouble and deal with the truth?" All we need to do is say, "Honey, tell me what to do?" Our wives can tell us plenty if we would just listen, and we would be doing ourselves a favor in the meantime.

It is the husband's responsibility to be the aggressor (not aggravator) in the decision-making policy of his home. Many men have become so slack in this area that they have turned it completely over to their wives. Husbands have appeased their wives to the extent that they, the heads of the home, make very few decisions. They leave it up to their wives to decide where they are going to go, what they are going to eat, when and where and with whom they will have their social lives. Of course, a man who does this can easily blame the wife when things don't work out, because he had been too weak to make the decisions himself and take the consequences upon his shoulders.

You may be one of those guys who feels sorry for himself, who says, "Well, I never get to do what I want to anyway, so why not let her do as she pleases?" All this time you think you are being so sweet, when in reality you are being weak. Why? Because you can't go through all the backlash of a disappointed and enraged wife. So you rationalize and say to yourself, "I'll let her go her way; then I'll be one up on her when I want sex activity or to go someplace with the boys."

One couple I know has worked out a good system in using divine order. Realizing that he must be the aggressor and make all the decisions within their home, he has given his wife the freedom to say what she feels and thinks. Then when he has listened carefully to her comments, he makes a decision. At the same time, when his wife becomes too aggressive in her approach, he says, "Honey, you need to back off." Thus they have a working principle that creates a loving relationship of giving and receiving yet recognizing the weakness of both parties. This is based on love and truth, so it adds to the peace and fulfillment of their home.

A wife feels fulfilled when she can advance her ideas and thoughts or criticism and observations freely to her husband, without his falling apart at the seams. If you are a good king, you will listen to the counsel of your department heads and then make your decisions, taking full responsiblity for all blunders. We men have such a hard time admitting our faults and bad decisions, that we generally rationalize or slough the fault off on our sweet wives.

God has given me a real feeling for the pressure we husbands place upon our wives because of our self-righteous attitudes. According to God's order, the wife is to be in subjection to the husband. But when he doesn't make the decisions, when he doesn't take things in hand, when he fails to be the spiritual leader, it causes undue anguish and hurt in the heart of his wife. As kings, you and I must handle our problems under the leadership of the Holy Spirit, looking squarely at the facts and truth under His light.

The characteristics of a Kingdom man, compiled in the Sermon on the Mount, are perhaps the best design for a new order of family living as well as the Kingdom of God. If you and I would follow this design in faith, by the help of the Holy Spirit, we would see a phenomenal change in every aspect of family life. Study Matthew 5-7 in the light of the Holy Spirit with your own kingdom (home) in mind and see if it doesn't bring new hope and happiness and holiness to your home.

Because God has given man "in Christ" the royal title of "Counselor," he needs himself to consult the Lord, to come before the court of His Lord to be given insight into the past, present, and future. Therefore, a husband must pray a lot. Formerly, in Israel, when a man went to consult God, he said, "Come, let us go to the seer" (I Samuel 9:9 Moffatt).

The main function of the husband, or prophet, is to receive, through the leading of the Holy Spirit, insight into every phase of family life. It is through prayer that we men are enabled to see the various needs of our wives and children. I have an idea that if I were to take a poll of men who are regular attenders at the Lord's house of worship and ask, "When is the last time you and your family got together and prayed?" I would get an answer like, "I don't know. It's probably been a long time. Besides, it's hard getting my family together alone for a period of time."

Be very careful to understand this mystery of prayer, for the lack of domestic tranquility leads to the failure of prayer to give you insight.

> *You husbands must be careful of your wives, being thoughtful of their needs and honoring them as the weaker sex. Remember that you and your wife are partners in receiving God's blessings, and if you don't treat her as you should, your prayers will not get ready answers (I Peter 3:7 TLB).*

As a prophet, you are a "seer," one to whom is given supernatural powers to "see" beyond the obvious to the spiritual and moral consequences of various actions and reactions of family activity. But if you do not treat your wife as you should and are not careful and thoughtful of her needs, then your role as prophet will be diminished because you will lose contact with the source of your wisdom and truth.

I must confess at this point that as a minister of a church, many times I am unable to receive the anointing because I am not treating my family right. I am hindered from receiving the truth and power of the Holy Spirit during the worship and preaching service because of my poor relationship with my wife and children. That is not the only reason that we ministers are not prophetic in our preaching, but it certainly contributes to much of the ineffectiveness of the pulpit in these times.

Your question at this point might be, "Well, I'm no preacher, so why talk with me about being a prophet or the ineffectiveness of the pulpit?" I must tell you that as the spiritual leader of your home, you become the preacher and the prophet. For you to function in this capacity, you must keep in contact with God the Father by prayer That contact is hindered when you don't treat your family right. It's that simple.

There are many causes for failure in prayer life, such as lack of faith and obedience and compassion and gratitude and love and forgiveness; also mental attitude sins like pride, worry, jealousy, fear, anger, hate, self-pity, mental adultery, stubbornness, rebellion; also lust-type sins like idolatry, witchcraft, passion of sex and drunkenness and murder and wild parties; also sins of the tongue like gossip, criticism, and foul language.

If you will notice, many of these causes for failure in prayer are very closely related to the domestic scene, the fury and fussing in the family. It falls on the shoulders of the chairman of the board, the husband, to bring order out of this chaos. This is a job for superman (supernatural), so it brings a man down to confession and repentance to prepare him to be filled with the Holy Spirit. When he is filled with the Holy Spirit, his head is anointed with oil (fellowship with the Lord) and his cup runs over (blessings overflow).

It is at this point that a man becomes the prophet in his family and can see with clarity the needs they have in the area of the spirit as well as the physical. It is easy to see when your children need new shoes or clothes or even toys, but it is much more difficult to see their psychological, social, emotional, and spiritual needs. This is especially true when you are blinded by your own selfish desires. However, when you are in God's divine order and are being obedient in faith, then you can "see" what those needs are and make arrangements for them to be dealt with. So many homes are in such need of husbands who will see to it that their wife and children are fed the proper spiritual food and that they pray and worship God together.

Being a prophet in your home will bring rich rewards. When you are able to tell what makes your wife happy, and to know what disappoints her, what motivates her, what helps her, what excites her, what aggravates her, what pleases her, what shames her, what delights her, and what gives her pleasure or joy or peace, then you are functioning as a prophet.

It is as a prophet that you know what kind of gift to give your wife. I heard one man say, "When my wife and I were first married, I would bring her gifts. But she always complained that they didn't fit or were the wrong color or in bad taste, so you know what?"

I said, "Yes, I know what. You stopped buying her gifts, and now you give her the money and tell her to go get it herself."

"That's right," he said, "but how did you know?"

"I know because I used to have that same attitude," I said.

"You mean you've changed your mind about it?" he asked.

"Yes," I replied. "Now I understand that as a prophet in my home, I must ask God to give me the insight to know what my wife likes and dislikes. I must study her like I would the characteristics of an animal I want to hunt or a fish I want to catch. I realize now that she is the most important catch of my life, and if I give it everything I've got, then the reward will be great."

He had a puzzled look on his face like I was a bit crazy, because he had always thought that once you caught your wife, once you had her down the aisle and a ring on her finger, you did not need to try any longer to catch her.

"I did all that stuff before we were married," he said, "but I'll be darned if I'm going to do it now."

If you, too, have this same attitude, you are truly missing out on the excitement and joy and challenge of being married. Where does it say in the marriage vow that you no longer have to look alive, be alive, and act alive? You are married until "death us do part" and "so long as ye both shall live." Death in the bad sense often occurs early in the marriage when we men stop trying, when we get upset with our wives and say "What's the we?"

There are many couples I know who are "dead" in that the husband has let their marriage die. They just haven't given it a funeral service yet. That is why so many marriages "stink"— because they are dead. When a man's attitude does not show any desire to make any effort to study and understand and please his wife, then the marriage is dead. I do not recommend divorce, I recommend resurrection. The purpose of this book is to bring back to life these thousands and thousands of marriages that are corpses. It is man's responsibility to initiate the resurrection. But he cannot do it by dying toward his wife, only by dying to self. Once self (the old man) is out of the way, then marriage comes back to life.

Remarriage is never the answer. God will see to it that you get another girl just like the one you had, so you might as well keep her and get rid of your old attitudes and sins and ego. If a man gets remarried and says, "Boy, this wife is so much better than that other one," he is just kidding himself. Before long the romance will be gone again, and he will be ready to trade her in for another new wife. This is not God's way of handling the matter, and the sooner we learn God's way, the better off our whole world will be.

There are a lot of men who want to get their wives committed to some mental institution so they can go get another wife and do the same thing to her. The reason so many wives are mentally off is because we men have actually driven them into this other world where they try to escape, but even there they are haunted by the echoes of sinful men down through the ages.

Many women are trying to escape their dead husbands by trying every new fad and fashion that comes along. But let's not blame them; let's face the truth and see that it is our attitude of selfishness that has caused this to happen. Men complain about their wives getting interested in spiritualism or witchcraft or all kinds of crazy activity, but let's face it— it is the men's fault.

Because we men are not the spiritual leaders, the prophets in our homes, we have allowed a gross injustice to occur, and all the while, we've made the women feel guilty when it is all our fault.

In the area of fatherhood, the prophet is able to see the needs of his children. The greatest need they have is a good example, because they are imitators. When they see in their Dad a great love and admiration for Mom, then they will repeat his example and respect her and him, too.

When a man is disciplined under the authority of the Holy Spirit, then he sets a good example. Otherwise, he becomes a poor example. If you are not disciplined enough yourself to do what needs to be done around the house and instead you waste time or you goof off, then how in the world are you going to expect your child to follow through? When the child comes home and he is supposed to do his homework, or supposed to do chores around the house, or supposed to practice, how can you expect your child to be self-disciplined when you are not self-disciplined? You cannot fool a child by saying one thing and doing another. Children pick up feelings, and they can feel when you resent your wife and rebel against her. And that child will grow up with these inner frelings of turmoil and strife and with resentment and rebellion, too. And he won't even know why. But it is because you have failed in your responsibility to take over and to do the things that you should be doing in your home, because you lack self-discipline.

I was interested in seeing what kind of response I would get from men who smoke, who are not self-disciplined enough to control when and where they smoke. So my wife and I invited about a dozen couples over to our house in which they had always before been allowed to smoke. But this time, as they arrived, we asked them not to smoke while in our home that evening.

There were all kinds of reactions. Some thought we were kidding. Some were indignant. Some kept on smoking. Some were quite uncomfortable. Some accepted the request and refrained from smoking until they got back in their cars.

The point I'm trying to make is this—you men who are unable to cope with change, or with rules and regulations, or with consideration of the rights or others because you lack self-discipline are going to set up very poor patterns of influence for your families.

There is only one way for a family to be permanently stabilized, and it is not by the husband making a fabulous salary. It is not by increasing your social activities. It is not by moving to the country or suburbs. It is not by wife-swapping. It is not in vacations, or clubs, or politics, or recreation. A family is permanently stabilized and joyous when the husband comes into the divine order, performing his office as the priest, the king, and the prophet in line with God's directions, living under the divine guidance of the Holy Spirit and principles of God's Word.

Many men are finding this to be true and are wondering why they rebelled so long, why they did not listen sooner, why this has not been taught, and why others are still trying different means.

Why wait any longer? Decide right now to come under the rule and reign of God the Father, so that you can become the right husband and right father for your family.

We are living in a day in which the homes are on the brink of disaster. Husbands and wives going in opposite directions. Children are rebelling against it all. The remedy is so simple—if men would change and become the priests and the kings and the prophets of their homes that God intended them to be.

The better you treat your family, the better the family. The opposite of that is true. The worse you treat them, the worse they are.

Husband, love your wife, treating her sacrificially in your love so much so that you are sensitive and aware of her needs as a responder. And give her love—love and more love. So do yourself a favor and love your own wife.

— TEN —

I Did Myself a Favor

The following thoughts came from a young man who has been exposed to the principles in this book:

Fred and I had arrived at the campfire late, for we had been playing pool in the recreation room located at the entrance of the campground. It was one of those coin-operated pool tables. We didn't want to waste our money, and we felt it wouldn't hurt anything if we came a little late to the meeting that had been prearranged to discuss family relationships in God's divine order.

Sure enough, the other men were already seated around the fire, which was well established and giving off a lot of heat. I felt sort of guilty as I sat down in the lawn chair, which someone else had brought for me to use. The kids were in another area with a young ministerial student, hopefully discussing the same thing around their campfire.

The conversation was well on its way, and it didn't take too long to get the drift of the message. As I sat there and listened to what the minister said, those hot sensations I felt didn't come from the campfire. It was a deep inward rebellion that was fighting its way to the surface, attacking the thoughts of this man whom I would have to list as my very best friend.

Had he joined the woman's lib movement? Gone over to the other side? Or was he under the influence of his wife? All kinds of thoughts went through my mind. I would not become henpecked, nor would I take the blame for all the things that went wrong in our house. This guy talked crazy, and the other guys were telling all their troubles without, I felt, giving all the facts, and asking Page, "Am I to blame?" And he always replied with, "Yes." I can remember his saying, as he told us of the divine order of God, "Husbands, love your wives, even as Christ also loved the Church, and *gave Himself for it.*"

I couldn't accept this bit about sacrificially loving your wife; it being my nature to be selfish. As we rode back to town that September afternoon, I wondered how many of the others felt like I did and how many felt like he did.

As time went by, we heard some sermons by Page on "God's Divine Order." I didn't realize it, but a lot of the doctrine Page preached before the camping trip and at the campfire had found a place in my memory bank, and I would recall it later as God's Word spoke to my heart.

I did myself a favor. I decided that I would, with God's help, put my household in God's divine order. I must confess that it is not as easy as it sounds, but it works. There have been times when I would not let Christ help me through my selfish nature and had to suffer the consequences. For instance:

We have a pecan tree in our backyard, and this fall it produced quite a few pecans. It was my "sanctimonious" idea to divide up the pecans evenly in number (ten-pound bags) to give to all our friends and relatives. My wife, on the other hand, felt that one of our aunts deserved a larger portion than the ten-pound bag because of her generosity to us over the years. I felt strongly about not showing partiality and so would not listen to my wife's plea to give this aunt more than I was giving others. My wife even offered to pay me for the extra pecans to give to her aunt, and this offended me, because these pecans were a gift of God, and I wasn't about to take any money for them—the very idea!

By this time, my wife was furious and in tears, and I was yelling at her, trying to get her to understand my position. So her we were, fighting over my pious position, and all the while I thought I was being the spiritual leader of my home. This went on all Sunday afternoon, our bickering back and forth about the pecans. I kept thinking "Something is wrong with my wife. How can se not see how 'good' I am, instead of insulting my spirituality?" After all, I had been to church that day and she hadn't, so that made me one up on her. I could not see it then, but it was clearly I who was out of order. My self-righteousness and self-pity came across like a foul odor, and no wonder my wife rebelled against me.

I have since realized that if my home is in discord, all the praying and worshipping in the world won't make me right with Jesus.

To know when your household is in divine order, each and every in fellowship with Jesus Christ and God, is a revelation. To not know it, is to experience self-pity, hate, and discord in and outside the household. I pray to my Lord and Savior that not only every man in our church, but in the community as well as the nation, would recognize through the Holy Spirit the divine order God has established, so we may praise Him and glorify Him in that order.

The above incident was used by permission, and we see mirrored in it our own selves. This episode was not at all funny to the family during the time it was happening, but as it is seen from outside, it is humorous—even to this family now after several months. One of the benefits of the Holy-Spirit-controlled home is being able to look at ourselves and our situation and see ourselves clearly enough to laugh, which is the cure of many of our homemade problems because so many of our problems are funny. That is why so many TV sketches are built around incidents that happen in the homes—they are medicine for our souls. We laugh and relax and enjoy the situation.

A cheerful heart does good like medicine, but a broken spirit makes one sick (Proverbs 17:22 TLB)

An instant replay of these funny incidents in our daily lives gives us plenty of funny material for making our hearts merry. If our hearts are merry, then we have the real medicine for making the home a happy one. There are limitless comedies and tragedies that occur every day in our living rooms, dens, bedrooms, kitchens, cars, and backyards. The sooner we learn, by the Holy Spirit, to be the "other people" rerunning these exciting scenes in Technicolor, the sooner we will be able to help ourselves. If what you see taking place is headed for a tragic ending, then talk with each other about it, face it, and resolve it. On the other hand, if it is funny, laugh and enjoy it. Most of the incidents in our family life deserve a big laugh. There are a few that deserve professional care. Learn to know the difference and act accordingly.

When a husband becomes aware that he is to be the spiritual leader in his home, then God the Father begins to really come alive for the entire family. The fruit that comes from a Jesus-controlled home produces a bumper crop. I knew a man whose eyes were opened to these truths, and the difference in that home was like day and night. He realized that if they were going to have any spiritual development, and consolation in Christ, any comfort of love, any fellowship of the Spirit, any tenderness of heart, and sympathetic understanding, any joy within the home—then he as the head of the home was going to have to change his attitude. He would have to humble himself, become obedient to the death principle of laying down his own ego, his own pride, his own stubbornness, and take up his role to be the prophet, priest, and king.

When he started admitting to his wife his mistakes, his unwillingness to read the Bible in the presence of his children, his unwillingness to pray in front of his wife, his embarrassment in going to church, his general disinterest in spiritual things, and when he started doing these things in the right spirit, there became a glorious openness and wonderful sweetness between him and his wife and children. They then began to see him as strong and loving and kind and helpful. When he would have decisions to make, he started including his family in on it by asking them go pray with him. They felt needed and drawn into one accord, working together for one purpose.

When his teenage son came home with temptations of difficulties, it was easy for him to talk with his father, because his father would reveal his own inadequacies and inability to cope from time to time, and together they would talk to the Lord, confessing that it was too big for them and that they needed His help.

The father really started being a godly father when he saw himself as one who was to help his wife and children grow in the Lord, that he was to encourage them and stimulate their love and dependence upon God, that he, as prophet, was to give them refreshment for their soul, that he was to help them grow in holiness and happiness and hope.

And now a word to you parents. Don't keep on scolding and nagging your children, making them angry and resentful. Rather, bring them up with loving discipline the Lord himself approves, with suggestions and godly advice (Ephesians 6:4 TLB)

Before, when a child of his wanted to talk, and he was busy watching TV or reading the paper or a book, he would tell the child to go play or talk with his mother. He did not realize that really what he was teaching was that God is too busy and really not interested in our needs as His children. This father and husband had thought of church as something to mess up his weekends—his time to be lazy or to be doing more exciting things like hunting, fishing, golfing, camping, watching TV, or going visiting. He never realized that his influence was so great that his children grew up dreading the weekends because it meant Dad and Mom getting in a fuss about church—or that terrible quietness when Dad and Mom didn't talk, or when they would go to church, but everybody was miserable, because Dad was miserable in his attitude.

Some of the men in my church have begun to understand what I have been teaching in this little book, and to their surprise, have found that their shaky marriages are becoming stabilized.

One young man, whose marriage had been in jeopardy, confessed to his wife his failure as a husband and then asked her to kneel with him beside the bed as they prayed together, holding hands, asking God the Holy Spirit to take control of their home. He began to realize that their family was sick because of his failure to lead in things pertaining to prayer, and reading God's Word and studying and worshipping with God's people. When a woman has to insist that her husband go with her to church, or read the Bible, or pray, it is no good. The man, the prophet, the head of the household, must take the initiative for it to be good. Otherwise, it is out of God's order, and the man rebels against it, and it becomes a farce. So this young man has caught the idea in leading in the spiritual matters of his home, and now all of the other problems and difficulties are beginning to fade away. His wife has fond a new respect for him; they can be honest with their feelings without it being a threat to their marriage; and their joy in the Lord has renewed that home to the point that other families have seen the difference.

I would like to use the words of John, a rather lengthy quotation, but one that I believe will set the mood for your desire to respond to the ideas and principles of this book. Men are basically skeptics; they want proof. It is true now, and it was true in the days of Jesus. But Jesus knew how to handle the doubts of men. He challenged them to try it, to test it, to give it a go. For those who did, what blessings were theirs! It can be so today with you if you will "give it a go."

Then the same day at evening, being the first day of the week, when the doors were shut where the disciples were assembled for fear of the Jews, came Jesus and stood in the midst, and saith unto them, Peace be unto you. And when he had so said, he shewed unto them his hands and his side. Then were the disciples glad, when they saw the Lord. Then said Jesus to them again, Peace be unto you: as my Father hath sent me, even so send I you. And when he had said this, he breathed on them, and saith unto them, Receive ye the Holy Ghost: Whose soever sins ye remit, they are remitted unto them; and whose soever sins ye retain, they are retained. But Thomas, one the the twelve, called Didymus, was not with them when Jesus came. The other disciples therefore said unto him, We have seen the Lord. But he said unto them, Except I shall see in his hands the print of the nails, and put my finger into the print of the nails, and thrust my hand into his side, I will not believe. And after eight days again his disciples were within, and Thomas with them: then came Jesus, the doors being shut, and stood in the midst, and said, Peace be unto you. Then saith he to Thomas, Reach hither thy finger, and behold my hands; and reach hither thy hand, and thrust it into my side; and be not faithless, but believing. And Thomas answered and said unto him, My Lord and my God. Jesus saith unto him, Thomas, because thou hast seen me, thou hast believed: blessed are they that have not seen, and yet have believed. And many other signs truly did Jesus in the presence of his disciples, which are not written in this book: But these are written, that ye might believe that Jesus is the Christ, the Son of God; and that believing ye might have life through his name (John 20:19-31 KJV).

Thomas, the doubter, was asking Jesus for His credentials. Thomas wanted proof of the peace; he wanted tangible evidence that this was truly the risen Lord before he would believe. This us understandable—it is what we men want. We do not want to go chasing some hypothetical bird in the bush. Most men are pragmatists; we have a built-in need to test the validity of something new. The attitude of Jesus to Thomas was, "Okay, Thomas, don't just be a spectator. Thrust your hand into my side; then believe." When Thomas saw that Jesus was no optical illusion, that Jesus was for real, then he counted Him worthy of his devotion and responded, "My Lord and my God."

This resurrection of Jesus was for real, and the same can be true for you and your marriage, if you will believe and then *act* on your faith. Jesus is perfectly willing to give us signs. In fact, He has already given ample signs. It is time now for you to get out of the grandstands and onto the playing field where you can become involved in your role as a spiritual leader of the home in being the priest, the king, and the prophet.

———■———

I feel the excitement, and a surge of joy wells up within my soul when I hear reports like that of the gentleman who said to me:

"Page, I never knew that life and marriage could be so terrific. Since I have come into this new understanding of the role of the husband as being the spiritual head of his wife, things have really been wonderful at my palace. I am so happy and so much at peace with the Lord, myself, and my family.

"Oh, I won't deny that we still have our fights—but what a difference, now that I understand that my wife is sent by God to help me, not to hurt me. I am so much more secure in my marriage, I can express my deep gut-feelings in all honesty with my wife, and even though sometimes she lashes back in fury, I have learned to cope, to hang in there and not feel threatened. And man, this horror I used to have with the finances is gone. I simply don't have to sweat it out anymore or fret and stew with my wife along lines of 'don't buy this' or 'don't go there.' I can relax and trust the Lord to supply our financial needs after my wife and I have knelt by the bed and prayed about it together with the Lord.

"And, man, you wouldn't believe the sex hang-ups we used to have—every night a hassle and a nightmare. Now since my wife has developed such a high respect for me in taking the home life in hand, she can't seem to show me enough of her love and affection. It's almost like that feeling we had when we were first married. And I have so much more freedom now that my wife doesn't have to suspect my actions anymore because she knows I'm faithful. There's no more hiding; it's all out in the open; and we hang loose and enjoy each other's company.

"If I've dome something wrong, I tell her. We work it out and move on, and she does the same with me. We don't mind exposing ourselves to each other, even though it often hurts, because there is a basic trust and love that sustains us in the Spirit, And we've learned how much sweeter it is to be honest with our feelings. I've learned not only to say what I think, but I've learned how to handle the feedback from my wife, which so often turns out to be a real exciting experience. There are fewer and fewer dull moments around our home, and we seem always to have tender and precious moments of silence, knowing that Jesus is present and sharing in our love for one another. I must confess that I never dreamed that life could be so meaningful and marvelous as I learned to change my attitude. With Christ as the head of our home, I have learned to trust in His promises and claim healing for my family and wisdom for the decisions.

"Page, I could go on and on, but I do want to thank you for introducing me to the happiest days of my life as I have found them in being freed from my self and attached to Jesus, the source of life. He has not let me down yet, and in His grace I have found by wife to be a true help-meet, perfectly suited for my every need. She was there all along, and I almost missed the greatest message for our day, 'Men, do yourself a favor and love your wives.'"

I am very pleased when men change their attitude about the Lord and themselves and their wives as this young man has done and hopefully thousands more will do in the coming days. It is my prayer that you will be among them.

This book has been written that you might believe in Jesus and His way of establishing a home. In so doing, you

165

will really do yourself a favor by loving your wife in the same way as Jesus loved the Church and gave Himself for it.

> *I know this is hare to understand, but it is an illustration of the way we are parts of the body of Christ. So again I say, a man must love his wife as a part of himself (Ephesians 5:32-33 TLB).*

God is so pleased when you become the prophet and the priest and the king in your own home. God is so pleased with that, that He will never, never allow the home to become divided or separated or destroyed, as long as you fulfill the divinely ordained responsibility that God has given you. When you are in line with the divine order, then God honors it and makes it a joyous home—a safe, exciting, enjoyable place for every member of the family. God takes care of the home and makes it heavenly.

> *If you want favor with both God and man, and a reputation for good judgment and common sense, then trust the Lord completely; don't ever trust yourself. In everything you do, put God first, and he will direct you and crown your efforts with success (Proverbs 3:4-6 TLB).*

———————■———————

I trust, Lord, that honor and peace and glory will come to my home as I begin to get in line with Your divine order, that is, You Lord, as my head, me as head of my wife, and me and my wife as head of our children. Lord, I am now willing to submit my will to Your will, and I thank You for the peace that passes all understanding. To God be the glory. Praise the Lord.

In the name of Christ Jesus,

Amen and amen